IN SEARCH
OF THE BLESSING

Gary Smalley
and John Trent, Ph.D.

A
JANET
THOMA
BOOK

THOMAS NELSON PUBLISHERS
Nashville

Published in Nashville, Tennessee, by Thomas Nelson, Inc.

Scripture quotations are from the NEW KING JAMES VERSION of the Bible. Copyright © 1979, 1980, 1982, Thomas Nelson, Inc., Publishers.

Scripture quotations taken from The Holy Bible: NEW INTERNATIONAL VERSION are marked (NIV) in the text. Copyright © 1973, 1978, 1984 by International Bible Society. Used by permission of Zondervan Publishing House. All rights reserved.

Scripture quotations taken from the REVISED STANDARD VERSION of the Bible are marked (RSV) in the text. Copyright © 1946, 1952, 1971, 1973 by the Division of Christian Education of the National Council of the Churches of Christ in the U.S.A. Used by permission.

Scripture quotations taken from THE NEW AMERICAN STANDARD BIBLE are marked throughout (NASB). Copyright © 1960, 1962, 1963, 1968, 1971, 1972, 1973, 1975, 1977 by The Lockman Foundation and are used by permission.

Library of Congress Cataloging-in-Publication Data

Smalley, Gary.
    In search of the blessing / by Gary Smalley, John Trent.
        p.   cm.
    ISBN 0-8407-4556-7
    1. Identification (Religion)—Meditations.   2. Devotional calendars.   3. Blessing and cursing—Meditations.   4. Love—Religious Aspects—Christianity—Meditations.   5. Parenting—Religious Aspects—Christianity—Meditations.   I. Trent, John T. II. Title.
BV4509.5.S63   1993
242'.2—dc20   92–39083
                                                                CIP

Printed in the United States of America
1 2 3 4 5 6 7 — 96 95 94 93

January

GOD'S OWN

> *"The LORD is my light and my salvation."*
> —PS. 27:1

Some children have a difficult time understanding the concept of a family blessing. They feel they have received a curse from a mother or father instead of a blessing.

Can such people ever move past this hurt and pain and feel genuinely loved and accepted?

If you had asked Helen this question four years ago, her answer would have been an emphatic no. In her mind, the pain she endured from a dysfunctional home had forever trapped her in a cycle of insecurity, fear, and unrest. Yet after years of anger, anxiety, and resentment, suddenly Helen discovered a way of escape. She began to understand and apply the very things you'll learn this month, principles that come right from God's love.

———————

Lord, thank You that You've promised to walk me through my hurt.

"Nevertheless, the LORD your God would not listen to Balaam, but the LORD your God turned the curse into a blessing for you because the LORD your God loves you."
—DEUT. 23:5

Have you felt, like Helen from yesterday, that you received a "curse" instead of a "blessing" from your parents? Let's learn a little more about the important words found in this verse.

The word *curse* is translated from the Hebrew word *qulalah,* which means "to esteem lightly, to dishonor." It is used of a "scanty" meal or a thin "trickle" of water—something to be despised, something not of high value.

Balaam was a sorcerer in the ancient Near East who was hired by a group of pagan kings to "curse" God's people. But he never was able to do it. God was not willing for His loved ones to be cursed. They carried great value as His children, children of a mighty God. So God turned Balaam's curse into a blessing for His people.

The same thing can happen for you, dear friend. We don't have to remain victims when the "restorer of our soul" can heal our hurt. In the days to come, you'll see how God can do this very thing for you.

Lord, thank You for a love stronger than any curse.

> *"My sheep hear My voice, and I know them, and they follow Me. And I give them eternal life, and they shall never perish; neither shall anyone snatch them out of My hand."* —JOHN 10:27–28

Many people who miss out on the blessing never feel secure in their relationship with their mother or father. In fact, some people are frozen in insecurity by their anger and hurt. In the next several days, let's look at how secure we can be in our Heavenly Father's love.

To begin with, Jesus gave His disciples (and us) a beautiful word picture of His constant care and concern. As the Good Shepherd, He was constantly talking to us through His Word and Spirit in His encouraging, familiar voice. And He gave us life eternal, the most important antidote to the most basic fear we all share: that of dying.

Jesus stressed that no one "shall snatch them out of my hand." This means we can be secure, even when we fail or we've been led astray.

Today, if you think back to a hurtful past caused by you or your parents, also think on this: the Good Shepherd is never asleep and never far from your side. You're in His hand today.

Lord, security comes from knowing You're with me till death—and beyond.

And Jesus came and spoke to them, saying, ". . . lo,
I am with you always, even to the end of the age."
—MATT. 28:18, 20

I'm never getting in an airplane again!" a seminary friend shouted out to me (John) one day, right in the middle of studying together at the library. "It's right here in the bible. There's no way we should ever get on a plane."

I couldn't believe my ears. I urged him to calm down and show me what he was talking about.

"Look right here, John," he said, pointing to today's verse. "It says, 'Lo, I am with you.' It doesn't say anything about *high*."

My friend laughed (and I actually did too) at this weak attempt at humor. But in reality, this verse gives us cause for great rejoicing, not humor.

Jesus told us here that He would be with us each day as the coming age unfolded. What a promise!

For those of us who may have come from difficult backgrounds, the security that comes from knowing He's always with us is tremendous.

No matter what our past may have held, and no matter how many future days we have, He stands beside us and loves us.

Thank You, Lord, that You're with us day in and day out, high or low!

> *"For He Himself has said, 'I will never desert you,*
> *nor will I ever forsake you,' so that we confidently*
> *say, 'The Lord is my helper, I will not be afraid.*
> *What shall man do to me?'*   —HEB. 13:5–6

The recipients of the book of Hebrews must have treasured these words of encouragement. Respected scholars note that the Hebrews who received this letter were hard-pressed with persecution on two sides. First, the Roman officials held them and the Lord Jesus they crucified in contempt. And second, many incompleted Jews (like Saul, before he became Paul) hated them as well!

When we're in the midst of persecution, the last thing we want is to have to face it alone. And the last thing that Jesus wants for us is to be lonely. There's no need! We have His personal promise that no matter who may have walked out on us in the past, He will never abandon us. He will never forget a birthday, a call, a commitment.

Because of that, we can have tremendous confidence before others, even before those who may seek to persecute us. People may try to cast us aside, but He is always and forever with us. We have His Word on it!

Lord, remind me that You are always by my side.

"He has sent Me to heal the brokenhearted."
—ISA. 61:1

The first thing Nancy had to face when she came home each night was whether her mother would be at the door with her coat on. If she was, it meant that her father was in such an angry mood that her mother, her brothers, and Nancy would have to go out and drive around until her dad was so drunk he'd passed out.

The children ate dinner and did their homework in the dim light of their car's backseat. They were never able to have friends come home to their house. They dreaded every holiday that promoted drinking to get in the "holiday spirit," because the "spirits" that grabbed her father caused his actions to be right from the pit.

Nancy grew up with a broken heart, shattered by anger, alcohol, and indifference. Yet, she learned in high school of Someone who could do the impossible.

Like a broken bottle, Nancy didn't even know where all the pieces of her broken heart lay. But when she came to know Jesus Christ, He gently began a mending process that has left her more secure, loved, and accepted than she ever thought possible.

God specializes in "binding up the brokenhearted." Others can help us, but Jesus can heal our hearts.

Thank You, Lord, that You can restore what was broken.

> *"He has sent Me . . .*
> *To proclaim liberty to captives,*
> *And freedom to prisoners."*
> —ISA. 61:1

Two years in solitary confinement. Leg irons shackled around your ankles fifteen hours a day. No light in your cell, except for the light from that one single bulb that comes on at dark and stays on until daybreak.

After more than 300 brutal interrogations, having your already broken leg deliberately snapped, being beaten in the face with a fan belt until you go into convulsions, and repeatedly being shown pictures of Jane Fonda leading protestors yet denied letters from your wife, you're only halfway through your 2,714 days in captivity!

For anyone else other than Captain James Stockdale, the senior officer of the infamous "Hanoi Hilton," such a situation would have led to despair. But this man, and others imprisoned with him, had a hope their captors couldn't crush. Prisoners smuggled Bible verses to each other and used a special code of coughing and shuffling to send prayers and words of encouragement from cell to cell.

Thankfully, most of us will never be in physical captivity. But all of us have been captives of sin, and some of us have experienced the control and captivity of a dysfunctional home. The strength that helped the heroes of Hanoi stay strong until their release can shelter us in God's love and free us from what chains us.

What freedom, oh Lord, to have You loose our chains.

"He has sent Me . . .
To comfort all who mourn."
—ISA. 6:12

It was a beautiful Thanksgiving day, and some family friends of ours (Cindy and John) were headed north to take a family picture. The mother, father and youngest child (a daughter) drove two hours to Sedona. Their three older sons flew to the gathering in a light plane, piloted by the oldest son. They had a wonderful family Thanksgiving feast at a resort restaurant and then snapped a picture of themselves with the famed red-rocks in the background.

After they took the picture, the father left to drive the mother and daughter home and the sons left in the plane. But his sons never reached their home. For an unknown reason, their plane crashed, and all three were killed.

What words would you share with this family? What words are there to share that wouldn't sound trite or empty?

As we talked to this precious mother on a Thanksgiving several years after this tragedy, we learned what had helped her hold on. It wasn't the words others spoke, she told us. "It was just a few friends *being there* to lean on. And knowing Jesus was there, too, even amidst the hurt."

Some of us have a heart full of hurt this day. All of us have a caring, responsive, quiet shoulder to lean on with the Lord Jesus.

Thank You, Jesus, that Your presence brings comfort and hope.

> *To comfort all who mourn,*
> *Giving them a garland instead of ashes."*
> —ISA. 61:3

Have you ever felt like a loser?

Bill played on a championship baseball team that won the title while he was pitching on the mound! As we talked with him years later, we discovered that day was a day of heartache, not of victory. Why?

Bill was the star hitter and pitcher on his team. Everyone in the league could see his talent, except his dad. Bill's father was driven to make his son the best, so he never praised him and never allowed him to think he'd done well at anything.

"During the championship game," Bill said, "we'd gotten a pretty big lead against the other team. So we began joking around in the dugout. Suddenly, my father walked over and yelled at me through the chainlink fence, telling me that he was leaving because I was acting like such a clown."

"I won the game," Bill said. "But I came home feeling like a loser."

Dear friend, we never have to feel like losers before God. In the Old Testament, a garland was given to the winner of a competition. All others got ashes. This verse describes God giving a garland to those grieving a loss. Even though they had experienced loss, God gave them a symbol of victory to show how He saw them—as winners.

Thank You Lord, that You see me as a winner.

"Giving them . . . the mantle of praise instead of a spirit of fainting."
—ISA. 61:3

The last thing Becky ever expected was to walk away from the test encouraged. But it actually shaped her whole life in a positive way!

Becky had a cleft pallet, and in the world of often merciless schoolchildren, she was made the brunt of many jokes. She was convinced no one could love her or that she would ever be successful.

Becky especially dreaded spelling bees. She went out on the first word, feeling self-conscious of her speech and appearance.

After one test, the teacher asked Becky to stay inside while the others went to recess.

"Becky," the teacher said. "You can spell those words, can't you."

Becky shook her head no first. Then slowly, under her teacher's gaze, she shook her head yes,.

"Honey," her teacher said, "I've always known you could do it. I'm already proud of you. Now next week, show the other children that you're proud of the talent God's given you."

Proud? Talented? Show the other kids?

Like the message of this day's verse, there is tremendous power in encouraging words. They can keep us from fainting and help us succeed. With the power of the teacher's encouraging words, Becky succeeded the next week!

———————

Oh Lord, Your encouraging words bring life and health to us.

> *"So they will be called oaks of righteousness,*
> *The planting of the LORD, that He may be glorified."*
> —ISA. 61:3

As a young boy, I marveled at it. As a teenager, I resented it. As an adult, I wondered at it again.

My (John's) mother grew up in a large house in Indiana, on several acres of land. The grounds looked huge to a little boy, but something else looked even bigger: the massive oak tree that stood on top of the hill, overlooking the house.

Ten of us youngsters holding hands couldn't have measured its circumference, and none of us could climb it. The first of its mighty branches was almost fifteen feet from the ground.

As a teenager, I hated the sight of the trees, particularly during leaf-raking season. It was still a beautiful site, but its fallen leaves created a back-breaking chore.

Today, nearly forty years since I first played at the foot of the tree, I marvel again at its endurance, steadfastness, and stamina. Three generations of my family grew up in the shadow of that tree, and we haven't touched its history. Those who trust in the Lord and who are planted securely in His garden are similar.

The many storms our tree has weathered are a testimony to its stability. And for those rooted in Christ, the winds of change and calamity will not shake the planting of God.

Thank You, Lord, that I have lasting roots in You.

"He is the same yesterday, today and forever."
—HEB. 13:8

For several days, we've been talking about security. If there is a deep-felt need in those who have missed the blessing, it's often a longing to be rooted and grounded.

Dave is a friend who spent a great deal of money purchasing a waterfront lot on a beautiful river. He put in his permit, and after months of waiting, he received permission to build a dock and dock-house to house his boat. He was presented with several options on how to anchor his dock. And he chose the cheapest and easiest.

That year, in the annual "once-every-twenty-year" flood, he lost his boat, dock, and dock-house!

It doesn't pay to skimp on what anchors us, particularly in the emotional and spiritual realm. It's crucial that we rely on the only thing that will keep us unmoved and unshaken.

Jesus Christ can provide the security we need because His strength, love, and compassion is unchanging, "yesterday, today and forever." What a promise for those of us who grew up with far too much change and uncertainty to gain a lasting sense of peace.

Lord, You are the anchor of my soul.

> *"Do not rebuke an older man, but exhort him as a father, younger men as brothers, older women as mothers, younger women as sisters, with all purity.*
> —1 TIM. 5:1–2

When we come to know Christ, we gain not only a secure relationship with our heavenly Father, but we join an entire family of brothers and sisters in Christ. These men and women can provide every element of the blessing to us, as well as communicate God's love, wisdom, and encouragement.

When Paul wrote to Timothy, he wasn't telling him that everyone in the church was related to him, physically. Rather, he was telling him that those who have the same spiritual Father share a close bond now, in this life, and will share eternity together.

For those of us who have come from a difficult background, meeting our spiritual family is a tremendous help and advantage. We may have never met our earthly father, but we can have a "spiritual" father come alongside and care for us in a special way.

Anne experienced this. Her own father had divorced her mother, and then passed away several years before her wedding. But she wasn't without someone to walk her down the aisle. Doug, the older "spiritual father" at work who led her to Christ, gladly did the honors.

Thank You, Lord, that You provide a spiritual family to help me grow.

"And He will love you and bless you and multiply you."

—DEUT. 7:13

We've seen how God can make a blessing out of a curse and how secure we are in Christ's love. We've even been reminded of the fact we have a spiritual family to re-parent us if we need it and to provide the love and support we need. But that's not all.

In this first month of the year when we look at how God looks at His own, we're looking through loving eyes. So for the rest of the month, let's get a clear look through "healthy" rose-colored glasses worn by the Rose of Sharon.

In the book of Deuteronomy, we read of a people coming out of exile who needed a clear sense of God's presence and promise. They received this promise when today's verse was spoken.

Notice this verse is not a conditional statement as claims of love often are today. "I may love you" or "I'll probably love you tomorrow," people say. But God clearly states that it's His will and intention to love you, bless you, and multiply you.

Lord, help me realize how deeply known and loved I am.

"The Lord delighted only in your fathers, to love them; and He chose their descendants after them, you above all peoples, as it is this day."
—DEUT. 10:15

Out of this, unfortunately, rarely studied book, comes another clear statement of how God looks at you—through loving eyes. God has a choice of whom to look at. And He chooses you, hands down.

A few weeks ago, a good friend received a large insurance settlement and set out to buy a new car. He knew just what car he wanted—color, make, and model. He had the money in hand, and he had fun at the car dealership, letting the sharks try to outdo themselves when they realized he had money and was buying today. Best of all, he was doing the choosing.

God has a choice. He didn't have to love the sometimes stubborn, hardhearted descendants of Abraham. But He did. And thankfully, He looks at our stubborn, selfish hearts and chooses us as well.

We may have been chosen last by parents or friends, but we can know what it's like to be a "first-choice" person with God.

What a joy to be chosen by You, dear Lord.

"I love You, O LORD, my strength."
—PS. 18:1

You've seen this plot in the movies. The bad guys are relentless at tracking the good guy down, until the tables turn. And because of the hero's cleverness, cunning, or sharp-shooting, the hunted becomes the hunter. The bad guys don't like this a bit.

Today's passage came right out of a similar story. This familiar Psalm was written by David during a time when he was the hunted. Saul and many enemies were trying everything they could to hunt him down. Yet, the instructions to this Psalm (which are actually part of the Hebrew text) tell us, "A Psalm of David the servant of the Lord, who spoke to the Lord the words of this song in the day that the Lord delivered him from the hand of all his enemies, and from the hand of Saul."

What did David say by way of praise and thanks? "I love Thee, O Lord, my strength."

Today, you may feel hunted by a memory or cornered by cruel circumstances. But you're not alone, and you don't have to be defeated. The same God who rescued David can bring you safely through your trials as well.

_____

O Lord, Your love energizes and sustains me!

I love the LORD, because He has heard
My voice and my supplications.
—PS. 116:1

We have a good friend who has five children and is fond of telling this favorite story.

It seems that it was dinner time, and his entire very talkative family were seated around the table. Everyone was talking at once, except the youngest son. Like watching a tennis match, he kept looking from one family member to another, waiting for some kind of opening or break in the conversation so he could get a word in edgewise.

Finally, frustrated beyond his endurance, he stood up on his chair and screamed at the top of his lungs.

Everyone instantly stopped talking, their eyes riveted on this child.

"What's the matter around here?" the boy shouted, "Doesn't anybody have any *ears?*"

Does this sound too close to home? Are there times when you feel you can't get a word of meaningful conversation spoken, or when you don't feel listened to.

Here in this Psalm, lies another great reason to rejoice in the love God has for us, for we're told He does hear our voice, even our supplications.

Lord, thank You for having ears that hear us whenever we speak.

Your name is ointment poured forth;
Therefore the virgins love you.
                    —SONG 1:3

Do you know how they used to purify oil in Jesus' day (and still do today if you travel to the Holy Land)?

One method was to take a series of trays and stack them, one on top of another. In the top tray would be a large stone. In the tray directly beneath it were smaller stones, and on down in size until the final tray was filled with fine gravel.

The unrefined olive oil was then poured through each layer of rock and gravel, so that all the impurities would be filtered out, and the pure oil collect at the bottom.

In the beautiful story and allegory of the Song of Solomon, Solomon's bride says why the maidens love him. It's because his "name" is like purified oil. His character is pure. So his love will be pure. Therein is another aspect of God's love, which we can draw strength from.

Jesus loves us in a pure, unhindered way. We will never again experience overcontrol or conditional acceptance. Christ's life was poured through the filters, making His love as pure as His character.

Your purity, Lord, makes us want to love You.

> *He brought me to the banqueting house,*
> *And his banner over me was love.*
> —SONG 2:4

Think back to junior high or high school. Did you ever go out on a date with someone you felt was very special, and then run into a bunch of his or her friends and had your date almost ignore you?

You can tell a great deal about what type of love a person has for you by how he or she treats you around others.

For Solomon, there was no doubt about his feelings for his bride-to-be. She told in the poem how he rolled out the banner when he stood beside her. He wasn't ashamed to be with her or embarrassed to associate with her. And therein is another powerful reason to be thankful for our God's love.

God's love for us leaves us no reason to feel ashamed. We may have been rejected by people in the past, but we're not rejected by Him today. He unfurls a banner of love that marks us out as specially His and specially loved.

_____

While others may have ignored or shamed us, Your love overshadows it all.

Many waters cannot quench love,
Nor can the floods drown it."
                    —SONG. 8:7

We can see another reflection of the character of God's love in today's verse. In a beautiful, poetic way, the flame of God's love is pictured as something no one or no thing can ever quench.

For many couples today, the flame of love has been turned down, or even extinguished. Yet, that doesn't have to be the case with us. Whether its the love that binds a couple together or the love that binds us to our Savior, Christlike love has an enduring, unchanging nature.

What a comfort to those of us who have experienced love based on a person's changing emotions rather than on a rock-solid commitment.

Robin needed love based on a commitment. Her mother left home when she was young, leaving her father to raise her and a deep emptiness in her heart. Yet, God's love finally helped her cope and conquer her loneliness. This love never went "downstream" nor saw its reality covered up.

Security grows as we realize Your love for us is inextinguishable.

> *If a man would give for love*
> *All the wealth of his house,*
> *It would be utterly despised.*
> —SONG 8:7

We just spoke of God's love being far too strong to be washed away by any floor or river. God's love is also priceless.

I (Gary) always carry a fake diamond to the Love Is a Decision seminars John and I teach. Even though the diamond is made only of cut glass, I enjoy holding it up and telling people that the price of that "diamond" is $100,000 and that it's for sale.

Each time I present the "diamond," I'm greeted with a number of laughs as people look at the oversized fake and shake their head at the price. But to me, the piece of glass is worth $100,000, because I've determined its worth! (I'm still waiting for that one buyer, though.)

The value we attach to something gives it its worth. We're told that if a man were to sell everything, the profits wouldn't come close to the price of God's love. And because God's love is priceless—we cannot afford to purchase it—He offers it to us as a free gift. People who try to buy God's love will be forever denied. Whatever they bring will be utterly despised because of the greater value of God's love. God's love is a free gift we cannot purchase.

Thank You, Lord, that Your priceless love comes freely to me.

"Who is a God like Thee . . .
He does not retain His anger forever,
Because He delights in unchanging love."
—MIC. 7:18

Change isn't always easy. Just ask Mike.

Mike's father was a salesman who worked for an aggressive, expanding company. That meant that his family was always moving—twelve times in his first fourteen years.

Different cities. Different schools. The need for new friends and for some sense of stability. Having lived everywhere, Mike didn't feel that any place was really home, except his church.

Amidst the myriad of adjustments, there was always a strong congregation in every city where Mike's family went. And though the scenery kept changing around him, God's love was unchanging. Knowing that made Mike secure.

Do you feel too ashamed over the sin of others or yourself to believe this truth? Don't be. We have a God who delights Himself in always being with us through any move we make!

_____

Lord, You always go ahead of me. Thank You.

Therefore the sisters sent to Him, saying, "Lord, behold, he whom You love is sick."

—JOHN 11:3

As we write this day's devotion, a close friend of ours lies in intensive care, recovering from major heart surgery.

Aged 46, with a ten month old baby, this wonderful Christian man is the last person we'd have expected to become sick. A former pro football player, he looked as if he were in the peak of health until his heart attack.

Like Lazarus' two sisters, who ran to Jesus, John and I (Gary) have done the same thing on behalf of our friend. God showed His power over death in raising Lazarus. It is our fervent prayer that our friend will also physically recover. Yet, unlike those who have no hope, we have a God who loves us, a God whose love isn't affected by life or death. Knowing our friend loves Jesus and Jesus loves him, we are encouraged that Jesus' love will sustain him through his recovery or his relocation to heaven.

What a comfort to know Your love stretches beyond death to life!

"A new commandment I give to you, that you love one another; as I have loved you, that you also love one another."

—JOHN 13:34

Madison Avenue long ago learned that people respond to certain key words when shopping. We like to have the latest and the best. So, once a year, it's almost guaranteed that the same old products we've been using will appear in bright, new packages, with the words "new and improved!" emblazoned on the sides. The "new" thing Jesus offered in today's verse, however, really made a difference in the world.

People in Christ's time were used to the rules, regulations and commandments of the Scribes and Pharisees. The Pharisees literally had hundreds of laws they had to observe each day. So lives were changed when Jesus introduced His new commandment to love one another, even as He demonstrated love—with agape love. This self-sacrificing love became the hallmark of genuine Christianity.

If you come from a home where there was little love, you can experience something "new"—God's love poured fresh on you daily, a love you can share with others.

Lord, we can have no greater model or challenge to love others than the life You lived.

> *"So they shall put My name on the children of Israel, and I will bless them."* —NUM. 6:27

Individuals and businesses proclaim ownership in various ways. Companies emboss their names on pens. Construction sites announce, "Future home of . . ." Sometimes people claim ownership to prevent trespassing or theft. Sometimes they do it as a symbol of pride.

God finds it just as important to show ownership of what He loves—to the world, to Satan, to all the forces against Him. God gives the name "Christian" to all who become a part of His family; all who love Him receive His "name."

Eric was orphaned at age ten and spent eight years bouncing between foster homes and orphanages. Several times, he was paraded before perspective "parents," but he was never once chosen. No one wanted to put their "name" on him. This crushed Eric.

Now in his thirties, Eric's burden has been lifted. He has become a new Christian and so has received God's family name, complete with God's blessing.

Children of all ages need Your blessing, and Your name upon them, O Lord.

But just as it is written,
"Things which eye has not seen and ear has not
heard,
And which have not entered the heart of man,
All that God has prepared for those who love Him"
—1 COR. 2:9 (NASB)

God's mysterious love stays forever fresh and welcome, even until the day we go to meet Him. Why is this "newness" in love important?

The familiar words "Familiarity breeds contempt" hold all too true in many relationships. Many couples we see in counseling, for example, have lost the freshness and warmth they had during their courtship. While they were dating, they longed to find out all they could about each other and to understand who they were and what they felt. Through the years, however, they have become indifferent, even angry at times.

God's love for us always has the positive element of courtship love—He never tires of knowing us or seeking to understand us. The verse that follows today's verse confirms this: "the Spirit searches all things, even the depths of God." God's Spirit pursues us endlessly on earth. And no ear, no eye can imagine the love we have in store for us in heaven.

Thank You, Lord, that Your love is ever as fresh and refreshing as spring.

> *"Nevertheless I have this against you, that you have left your first love. Remember therefore from where you have fallen; repent and do the first works."*
>
> —REV. 2:4–5

Yesterday, we saw that God's love carries a mystery and depth to it that keeps it always fresh. Today, we read how we can rekindle that love should it sputter on our part.

As God disciplines the Ephesian church, He points out that they have left their "first love." Yet, He gives them a plan for restoring that love.

1) *Remember, therefore, from where you have fallen,* He says. Think back to the many things you used to appreciate about each other.

2) *Repent.* Turn away from those things that are weakening your relationships and back to what strengthens them.

3) *And do the deeds you did at first.* Get back to doing those small, specific, positive actions that were so natural when your love was new and fresh.

Lord, even if I wander, thank You that I can rekindle that "first love" for You in my heart.

"For God has not given us a spirit of fear, but of power and of love and of a sound mind."
—2 TIM. 1:7

If you've read each devotion this month, then you've got nearly thirty reasons to feel loved and blessed by God! God desires to bless you. It's His purpose in creating you. He delights in doing it, even if it means lifting and removing a curse from your past.

Some of us have been so badly hurt, however, we can't "feel" God's love. We are still caught in the fear created by our pain.

In today's verse, we see the great truth that God has not given us a spirit of fear. Someone in the past may have instilled fear in our lives, but not Jesus. In 1 John 4:2, we're told that "Perfect love casts out fear." Jesus' love is perfect; it is strong enough to cast out fear.

If we want to become less loving and less likely to feel God's love, we can hold onto our fear. We can simply reverse the equation of 1 John and get, "Fear can cast out mature love."

Jesus' love gives us the power and perspective we need to feel His love, and to pass it on to others.

———————

Thank You, Lord, that I can change and grow in Your love.

> *"The LORD's mercies*
> *are new every morning;*
> *Great is Your faithfulness."*
> —LAM. 3:23

As part of my (John's) doctoral training, I worked at a psychiatric hospital. Perhaps the most difficult thing for me there was trying to understand and encourage those people who saw no hope in even getting out of bed. These people were emotionally beaten down. The mere thought of facing a bright, new shining day was almost too much for them to bear.

What can help us experience the love we've written about all month? What can give us that reason to get up in the morning, despite our struggles or difficulties?

One verse that I shared repeatedly with those who had lost hope was today's selection. Despite our trials or past, we all have a glorious future, every morning, because of God's faithfulness.

As you read through the rest of this devotional, remember that each day's reading comes complete with a dose of God's mercy based on a changeless, precious love, and kept certain by His faithfulness.

Dear Lord, thank You for giving me that reason I need to go on victoriously.

"In Him you also trusted, after you heard the word of truth, the gospel of your salvation; in whom also having believed, you were sealed with the Holy Spirit of promise."

—EPH. 1:13

Soldiers who are separated from their families look forward most to one thing—mail-call. That is the time they hope to find a little bit of home scribbled on a piece of paper and stuffed inside an envelope, sealed and sent with love across the world to where they are.

The person who knows Christ bears a seal like the envelope the soldier awaits. After having heard and believed the Gospel, our souls are sealed with the mark of God's Spirit. We can't see this from the outside, but God can see it on the inside. And like that envelope that may travel across the world to reach its destination, so our hearts are safely sealed and kept by God's Spirit.

When the "day of redemption" comes for us all, there will be a roll call of names. And not one of God's children, you included, need worry that the "mail's been lost." We're sealed in God's Spirit until we're delivered at the doorway to Heaven.

What encouragement You bring us, O Lord, on the days we most need it.

> *And do not be conformed to this world, but be*
> *transformed by the renewing of your mind, that you*
> *may prove what is that good and acceptable and*
> *perfect will of God.*
> —ROM. 12:2

Earlier this month we looked at the great blessings that are ours. Charles Dickens saw beyond his day and wrote these lines from "Things That Never Die," a poem as fresh as tomorrow and an inspiration for today.

> *Let nothing pass, for every hand*
> *Must find some work to do,*
> *Lose not a chance to waken love—*
> *Be firm and just and true.*
> *So shall a light that cannot fade*
> *Beam on thee from on high,*
> *And angel voices say to thee—*
> *"These Things shall never die."*

Lord, may my mind and heart be transformed according to Your perfect will.

February

LAYING CLAIM

> *Bless the Lord, O my soul; and all that is within me, bless His holy name!*
> —PS. 103:1

One of the most beautiful things about the Bible is the repetition of the promises God makes to bless His people. Perhaps nowhere are these promises capsulized so well into a single chapter as into this psalm that touches every aspect of our lives.

This month we will concentrate solely on the 103rd Psalm. Each day we will examine a verse, or in many cases, part of a verse, then discuss the blessing, the promise, or the inspiration it offers. Stories of those who have claimed these promises can also encourage us to claim them.

Why concentrate so much on "blessings"? The word itself tells us why! In Hebrew, it literally means, "to bow the knee." Today, few people, other than orchestra conductors or debutantes, "bow" their knees. But in Old Testament times, it was common to bow before someone of great worth and value.

Can you see now how God looks at you? When He blesses you, He's saying that you're of great worth and value. And when we "bless the Lord," we're saying He's of highest value.

Bless the Lord, O my soul, with all that is within me.

Bless the Lord, O my soul, and forget not all
His benefits. —PS. 103:2

During the span of years allotted to each of us, we often say, "I will never forget this as long as I live." In reality, we do forget—joys and sorrows, experiences with God. We vow always to remember, but our memories often fade.

The ability to remember God's benefits is a blessing in itself! How joyously we could live if we remembered all our times with Him and not just those mountaintop moments! More and more, Christians are turning to journaling. Unwilling to trust faulty memories, they record deep thoughts, new insights, answers to prayers, and family experiences.

It has been said that the weakest ink is stronger than the best memory. Getting down on paper the things we want to relive is a marvelous blessing to ourselves and to our families. One man in a senior center writing class shared, "It doesn't matter if my book sells. When I read it, I meet long-gone friends and get to experience those years again."

O Lord, teach me to remember all Your benefits.

> *[God] forgives all your iniquities.*
> —PS. 103:3

A wonderful promise to remember today is that God forgives not some, but *all* our iniquities.

Dan had a father with a terrific memory for everything he did wrong. For years, even after his father died, he still struggled with making any kind of mistake. When he did stumble in any way, he was incredibly hard on himself. Yet, when the freedom of this verse really hit him as truth in a counseling session, he literally cried tears of relief. The same freedom he felt is available to you as well.

The Christian media features people who, at their lowest point, turned to Jesus and found forgiveness and peace. Sometimes God allows a person to reach Death Row before finding Him. Yet once God is found, the offender is pardoned in heaven, though perhaps not on earth. Sometimes, however, God permits that person to remain here long enough to tell the world of his unworthiness and of God's unexplainable forgiveness for all who seek Him and request it.

Is there a sin, an iniquity, in your life you've thought God couldn't forgive?

Thank You, Lord, for the blessing of forgiveness—for me and all who ask.

[God] heals all your diseases.
—PS. 103:3

A man whose wife died despite a surgeon's best efforts was bitter. "I thought God healed people. My wife spent her whole life trusting and serving Him and He lets her die when she isn't even fifty! Why didn't He heal her? Everyone we know prayed for her."

This man expressed the age-old cry, "Why, God? Why are some healed and others not?" When the psalmist said, "God heals our diseases," shouldn't he have added, "but not all the time"?

A friend of the grieving man had a different thought. "Your wife has been healed. We don't like to face death as the ultimate healing, but it's the truth."

As followers of our Lord, we aren't exempt from the loss of loved ones from disease. We are, however, assured of that ultimate healing. It's no Mommy-kiss-it-and-make-it-well panacea, but God's final answer to hurts. At times, God does save those the doctors have pronounced incurable, but He is no less almighty or caring when He does not restore us to earthly health.

God, thank You for Your healing. Please help me to accept Your method.

> *[God] redeems your life from destruction.*
> —PS. 103:4

Jack was out of work and had to support his family by selling his family treasures. Last to go was the watch Jack's grandfather had given him as a teen.

"Don't sell it," Jack pleaded with the pawnshop owner. "As soon as I get the money, I'll come for it."

"You know the rules," the man snapped. "Thirty days is the limit. After that . . ." He shrugged. "If someone wants to buy it, you're out of luck, mister."

Jack found work, and before the grace period ended, he redeemed his watch.

In order for something (or someone) to be redeemed, that object or person *must first have belonged to the one redeeming it.* Only the real owner has the right to free what has passed from his possession.

Today, take a moment to think about the cost Jesus paid to redeem you. It took His blood, His tears, and His very life. But He laid it down voluntarily for you because He loves you.

Jesus, You are my redeemer. I praise You, Lord.

[God] crowns you with lovingkindness.
—PS. 103:4

What a beautiful word, *lovingkindness*. The two parts show such goodness and caring on the part of our Heavenly Father. Suppose that every child of God wore the crown of lovingkindness. Not for personal glory or blessing, but for the benefit of others.

Some do. They are the ones who go far beyond themselves in serving and blessing others.

Anne Sullivan came to Helen Keller when the almost-seven-year-old, deaf-mute could only kick and make choked sounds to vent her frustration at her prison. Anne's crown of lovingkindness survived incredible obstacles, yet she stayed with Helen Keller until death. Her devotion has enhanced innumerable lives.

Mother Teresa, too, has passed on lovingkindness to the poor and the lepers of India. Her awards received, including the 1979 Nobel Peace Prize, are recognized by others as the crown of lovingkindness she wears.

Lord, how can I show lovingkindness today, and to whom?

> *[God] satisfies your mouth with good things.*
> —PS. 103:5

Food is a basic need for human survival. The Bible describes many times God provided food when His children (and others) needed it: the wandering Hebrews, Elijah, the five thousand.

And feeding miracles aren't limited to Scripture. God blesses hungry people in a variety of ways. Sometimes imprisoned saints, in modern godless countries, have discovered God's provision through compassionate guards. At other times, He has stretched what little bit one person shared until the needy were fed enough to hold out.

One of the most loved pieces of poetry ever written is James Russell Lowell's, "The Vision of Sir Launfal." What a lesson it has for us about the importance of being part of a chain of blessing by helping to feed those who have not.

> *Not what we give, but what we share,—*
> *For the gift without the giver is bare;*
> *Who gives himself with his alms feeds three,—*
> *Himself, his hungering neighbor, and Me.*

God, help me not just to give, but to share myself and my blessings.

Your youth is renewed like the eagle's.
—PS. 103:5

Sarah's life of turmoil changed when, after years of enduring her husband's alcoholism and infidelity, he finally died. Although still in her forties, she looked and felt old enough to be a great-grandmother.

Months passed and Sarah met a wonderful Christian man who offered her love, acceptance and a greater joy than she could remember. They fell in love. Unwilling to enter a new marriage until she knew God's will, they waited. Sarah appreciated his patience in allowing her time to fully heal. At last they became engaged.

"I feel like a young girl again," Sarah told a friend. The compassion and caring of her husband-to-be had renewed Sarah and her face shone with youth and eagerness.

Is there a time in your life when you experienced the blessing of renewal? Do you need to be renewed now? Bruised and hurting from life's crazy up and down swings, we need to both receive and give renewal.

God, please renew me, and help me to pass it on to others.

The Lord executes righteousness.
—PS. 103:6

Personal righteousness should be the goal of every child of God, regardless of age or social status. However, we must not be hesitant to make a statement or join a church until we achieve a high degree of righteousness. When we hesitate, we bypass the fact that God Himself executes righteousness and that once we have taken those first trembling steps, He helps us walk steadily.

A good friend experienced this truth. This man knew Christ but didn't want to join a church because of his smoking habit. He wrestled with it and finally approached the minister, who encouraged him by saying, "Take the first step. God will help you with the second." The man came out of the waters of baptism and from that day has never had even the desire to smoke. God blessed him with a degree of the righteousness he longed to possess.

Oh, Lord, execute righteousness on my behalf, that I may follow

*The Lord executes . . . justice for all who are
oppressed.* —PS. 103:6

Often when we think of the oppressed, we think of minorities, those from unfamiliar cultures who live in nonaccepting societies. There are many more oppressed people than these obvious ones: the downtrodden poor, the abused child, the battered spouse, the debt-ridden single parent, the struggling minister fighting apathy or congregational strife.

The word *justice* brings to mind a Supreme Court Justice or a Justice of the Peace. What did David mean when he promised that God brings justice to all who are oppressed?

Justice is closely akin to righteousness in that it implies fair and impartial treatment for those who seek a moral answer. Just as physical healing doesn't always come when we pray, neither does justice. Think of martyred saints, persecuted Christians, those who face bigotry and prejudice, and we have to admit, life simply isn't always fair. Our hope lies in the fact that one day justice will rule.

Lord, help me actively seek to bring the blessing of justice—now

> *He made known His ways to Moses, His acts to the*
> *children of Israel.*
> —PS. 103:7

The most blessed people on earth are those who bless others. Likewise, God delights in blessing us, for He in turn, receives our blessings.

Have you ever considered Moses and the children of Israel being so important to God that He made known His ways and His acts? God isn't required to explain His will or self to anyone. He is God, Supreme, All Powerful. Yet He knows His children are strengthened when He makes His ways known to them.

That's what happened to Ted one day, as he sat on his lake-front porch. While watching a beautiful sunrise, a sense of awe settled over him like a warm blanket. For the first time in years, a sense of heartache began to lift off of him as the truth of a single verse in God's Word hit him.

"For years, I'd struggled over losing my wife. I was lonely and bitter. But then it came to me while watching that sunrise. The truth of the verse, 'Thy mercies are new every morning; great is Thy faithfulness.' God hadn't left me alone. He was giving me a picture of His presence in every sunrise."

Thank You, Lord, for making Your ways known to me.

The Lord is merciful.
—PS. 103:8

One of the most highly decorated soldiers of the Civil War was the North's General Chamberlain. He received the Medal of Honor for bravery, had nine horses shot out from under him, and was wounded numerous times.

He was so respected by Lincoln, General Grant, and all the Union soldiers, that his division (the 1st Maine), was designated the honor guard when General Lee surrendered at Appomatox Courthouse.

When the surrender was completed, and General Lee began to ride down the road flanked on both sides with Union soldiers, some began to laugh and jeer. But General Chamberlain rode down the line, silencing his men. Then he ordering every man to stand at attention, present arms, and salute in honor their greatest foe. An uncompromising warrior in battle, Chamberlain was also gracious and merciful in victory.

Do you model mercy in your life? Children who grow up in highly authoritarian homes often do not learn how to be merciful because thy do not see mercy practiced. However, we can turn to our Heavenly Father to help us develop mercy in our own lives and in our children's lives.

One definition of mercy is, "a blessing that is an act of divine favor or compassion." As you go about your day today, consider God's mercy.

By Your mercies, Lord, I am blessed and made whole.

The Lord is . . . gracious.
—PS. 103:8

A high school principal described a highly respected teacher. "She is both efficient and gracious; one of the few real ladies I have been privileged to know."

I found it surprising to discover the first Webster definition of *gracious* was "godly," but it was marked obsolete; "Pleasing" and "acceptable" were listed as archaic. The current descriptions include "marked by kindness, courtesy, tact and delicacy." Too bad we didn't keep godly as the number one definition.

Amy grew up in a home where few kind words were ever spoken. Her father used profanity the way sailors do at sea, and her mother always had a rough edge to her voice.

Angry words were so frequent and out-of-balance, that even at a young age, Amy decided that in her home, things would be different—and they are. Her speech, tone of voice and gracious manner are a reflection of the God she loves, not the words she'd heard.

God, may I grow in graciousness by Your example to me.

The Lord is . . . slow to anger
—PS. 103:8

Alexander Pope went straight to the heart of life when he wrote, "To err is human, to forgive, divine." On this Valentine's Day when hearts and flowers say, "I love you," there is no better time to remember God's patient, forgiving love.

Uncontrolled anger is in direct contrast with patience and forgiveness. Homes filled with shouting matches or violent arguments leave indelible scars, setting up negative patterns for future generations. Is it any wonder that the Scripture cautions against sudden, uncontrolled anger?

One day while disciplining her children, Milly discovered she sounded just like her own mother had, years before. Her shrill accusations, refusal to listen, and urge to strike out were a mirror image of what she had lived through and vowed never to allow in her own home.

God wants to teach us control. We can learn more rapidly by picturing, in our calmer moments, the way we want to respond to family problems, and commit ourselves to these more positive responses.

Lord, may I be freed from anger and filled with love throughout this day.

He has not dealt with us according to our sins, nor punished us according to our iniquities.

—PS. 103:10

Amazing grace! How sweet the sound!
That saved a wretch like me!
I once was lost, but now am found;
Was blind, but now I see.

John Newton's cry of praise for freedom from the iniquity of being a slaver has echoed down through the years, in agreement with the psalmist. When Newton accepted Christ into his life, he broke stronger chains of bondage than those that bound his captives.

When we think of law and justice, we believe that the punishment should fit the crime. Yet God's laws and His justice are not chained to human understanding. Once we accept the grace and sacrifice of our Lord Jesus Christ, we are freed from all blame in God's eyes.

How different God is from parents who withhold the blessing of approval, often even love, from disobedient children. Thank God that even when we are not worthy of His blessings, He still loves us, and bestows peace, joy, and happiness.

O Lord, I thank You that You offer me unconditional love.

*For as the heavens are high above the earth, so
great is His mercy toward those who fear Him.*
—PS. 103:11

Commitment is costly. If you are serious about com-
mitting yourself to blessing those you love, expect to
pay a price, though not necessarily in monetary terms.
Rather, think in terms of the time, energy, and effort
you will need to invest to see the blessing become a
reality in their lives.*

Are you finding it hard to make or to keep such a
commitment? The help offered in Psalm 103:11 is real
and practical. God's mercy toward those who fear Him
is as great as the heavens are high above the earth!
Take a moment on a clear day to gaze upward. It is
impossible to grasp how high the heavens are, or how
far-reaching.

God has committed Himself to blessing us and showing us mercy. Just so, we can commit to blessing and
showing mercy. God is a perfect model.

What a wonder that the same God who controls
wind and wave, thunder and lightning, stoops to have
mercy on us.

———————

Lord, Your endless blessings are truly heaven high.
*THE BLESSING, Chapter 7

> *As far as the east from the west, So far has He*
> *removed our transgressions from us.*
> —PS. 103:12

I wish I could walk away from everything I am," a teenager told her mother. "I'm seventeen years old and my life is one big mess. I overeat then hate myself, no one likes me at school and all you and Dad do is yell at me."

Can you relate? If the teenager could remove what she feels she is, as far as the east from the west, how free would she feel? Isn't it great to know God snatches up our transgressions and ships them off to the other side of the world?

Are you burdened with the weight of past mistakes? Try this exercise. Picture each transgression wrapped for shipping, strapped and taped, so it cannot break loose. Visualize a whole bundle of them being tumbled into the hold of a great ship with the name **GOD'S MERCY** blazoned in enormous letters on the hull. See that ship sail away carrying your transgressions away until they can never return. Do you feel free and pardoned?

I bid a final farewell to my transgressions and accept freedom, my God.

*As a father pities his children, so the Lord pities
those who fear Him.*   —PS. 103:13

Gail remembers a crucial day in her transition from
child to woman. When the first boy she ever really
cared about fell for her best friend, Gail turned to her
father for comfort. Instead of showing pity, love or
even much interest, he laughed and said every teenager had to go through it.

"I didn't need to hear his laughter," Gail says. "I
needed him to listen to me."

Is there someone in your life who needs your pity
and understanding, even as you need the Lord's?

Emily Dickinson wrote from the depths of pity for
an aching world.

> *If I can stop one heart from breaking,*
> *I shall not live in vain;*
> *If I can ease one life the aching,*
> *Or cool one pain,*
> *Or help one fainting robin*
> *Unto his nest again,*
> *I shall not live in vain.*

She also wrote from the God-given sense of responsibility each of us who bear His name and His cross
must have for the needs of others.

Bless me with the gift of accepting others' needs, please, Lord.

*For He knows our frame; He remembers that we
are dust.*   —PS. 103:14

It's encouraging that God's wisdom takes into consideration our humanness. Not that He excuses us when we deliberately choose the wrong path. His nature won't permit that. Yet, He offers us an acceptance we can pass on to others and continues to lead us in love.

When Diane was born, her parents saw that her left arm had never developed below the elbow. Leaving tears behind, her parents thanked God that Diane had no other serious problems. Then, with Diane nestled in her mother's arms, her parents prayed that their love would make up for any physical disabilities she possessed. They vowed to encourage Diane to become all God would have her be. In other words, they knew her "frame" with its frailties and focused on the high value of the child, not her weakness.

Diane grew up secure, accepting herself.* Is there something about yourself you need to accept, even as God has accepted it?

Lord, help me to see myself as You see me and to know Your acceptance.

*The Blessing, Chapter 5

As for man, his days are like grass.
—PS. 103:15

The summer of 1992 brought a startling upset for the normally rainy (and green!) city of Seattle. Because of an unusually low snow pack, Seattle residents found themselves in a water crisis such as they'd only thought happened in the "dry" states, like California and Arizona.

"No lawn watering," came the mandate. "No flower and garden watering with hoses. Conserve." TV stations carried suggestions on how to cut down on water usage.

Grass throughout the city browned. Yet, the grass roots still had the moisture from deep underground and lived. With the fall rains, the burned grass became green again.

We can be like "Seattle" grass. If we are rooted in the well of God's blessings, we will have something to cling to when the arid days come and we'll always be ready to thrive.

God, I know Your blessings are always there, even when I don't feel them. Please help me stay rooted in You, even in the dry times.

*For the wind passes over it [the flower], and it is
gone, and its place remembers it no more.*
—PS. 103:16

A lady who grows beautiful roses was asked which she favored.

"I know of no rose more beautiful than the Chicago Peace," she said. "Yet on hot days they appear as buds in the cool morning, open quickly to the sun, are full-blown by evening, then usually wilt. They don't have any stamina. We can only enjoy them for a short time.

"Other roses, like the Precious Platinum, last in the house or out, through heat, rain and wind, sometimes up to a whole week. They don't drop their petals until every one is ready to fall at once in a neat little pile. Perhaps they aren't as delicate as the Peace varieties, but I admire their endurance and continuing beauty."

Are you a Chicago Peace? Or a Precious Platinum? Has God blessed you with rare beauty and delicacy, a subtle perfume? Or are you sturdier, given the gift of facing the elements and still giving your best that those about you may be blessed?

We are all beautiful in Your sight. Thank You, Lord.

But the mercy of the Lord is from everlasting to everlasting on those who fear Him.
—PS. 103:17

The birthday of George Washington is no longer a legal holiday. The passing of years has dimmed some of the respect we once held for "the father of our country." However, time can't erase his prayers.

"I hope I shall always possess firmness and virtue enough to maintain what I consider the most enviable of all titles, the character of an honest man," characterizes the aspirations of this practical but visionary man. Note the word *always*.

As far as we know, he died still cherishing honesty and truth. He knew the everlasting mercy of the Lord Who lives and reigns without beginning or end.

Thinking about a creation that has no beginning or end can leave your head spinning. We can't, now, comprehend our Lord's infinite, everlasting character—or His everlasting mercy, but one day we will.

Please bless me, Lord, with an understanding of Your everlasting mercy.

His righteousness [is] to [His] children's children.
—PS. 103:17

An Old Testament blessing was not only to the one who received the laying on of hands, but also to all his descendants. The blessing was to travel down through the generations, strengthening and sustaining all who received it.

Orthodox Jewish homes continue to practice family blessing. Millions of Christians bow their heads each week to receive a benediction, a sending forth prayer. These blessings are designed to not only close a specific worship experience but to give something for the worshipers to take home with them and treasure throughout the week.

One of the most effective blessing experiences you can have is to be part of a prayer circle. The joined hands make physical contact and the prayers sweep through the circle like a wind. Consider starting a prayer circle in your family, allowing the blessing to travel from person to person, generation to generation.

Lord, I pray for Your righteousness, for me and my family. May we pass it on in prayer.

To such as keep His covenant, and to those who remember His commandments to do them [mercy and righteousness].　　　　　　　　—PS. 103:18

One of the most comforting things about our relationship with God is the assurance He won't let us down—*ever.* When we become His children, we make an everlasting covenant with Him. Even when at times we fail Him, God still keeps His part.

We can boldly claim God's promises of daily blessings for those who keep His covenant and obey His commandments.

What is your greatest need today? A blessing of words? Turn to your Bible. A blessing of touch? Then see if you can pass on part of the blessing with a hug for someone. Perhaps you need the blessing of knowing God's esteem for you, or His mercy and righteousness. Again, turn to your Bible. How valuable we must be for God, Creator of all, to send His Son for us!

Have you made a commitment, or are you keeping your commitment to God? He is committed to you.

May I receive Your blessing, Father, as I keep faith with You.

The Lord has established His throne in heaven, and His kingdom rules over all. —PS. 103:19

Many of us picture God as a kindly, grandfatherly man with a flowing beard and a lap big enough for everyone in the world to climb into. However, one lady said she never dared climb into God's lap, even in her dreams. Instead, she always brought a little footstool when she approached God. She placed it as close as she could get to His glittering throne, sat on it, and leaned against God. She knew He would never move away and leave her sitting there alone and lonely.

Were you a child whose parents never had time to listen to you or hug you? Did your toys remain broken?

Deep down, you may still have an empty spot from some such sin of omission on the part of your family. Turn your thoughts to God, whose heavenly throne is open to all, no appointments necessary. His kingdom rules over all. God can fill that empty spot with His love. God is never too busy for you, and nothing is too trivial for Him.

How thankful I am, God, that Your love fills all my emptiness.

Bless the Lord, you His angels, who excel in strength, who do His word, heeding the voice of His word.
—PS. 103:20

There are many references to angels in the Bible. We find them engaged in all types of activities. One wrestled with Jacob. Others announced special coming events. Still others rejoiced in the return of a lost sheep to the fold, or a sinner who repented.

Billy Graham's book *Angels* became an instant best-seller. Why? Because people, even those not God's own, want to know more about these heavenly beings. (Who isn't impressed when people receive miraculous help from a source unknown and impossible to identify?)

Dr. Graham testified in the closing chapter of his book that, as he had yielded his will and committed himself unreservedly to Christ, God placed a hedge of angels to protect him.

Can you imagine what life could be if all who follow Jesus lived with the absolute knowledge that angelic ministry is available? What great blessings would be possible.

God, hedge me in with Your angels and protect me this day.

> *Bless the Lord, all you His hosts, you ministers of*
> *His, who do His pleasure.* —PS. 103:21

Are you guilty, as most of us are from time to time, of viewing ordained ministers as the only ones who are to spread the gospel and comfort the sick and dying? This is a common fallacy that is becoming obsolete. Yes, there will always be such ministers who are specially called and set apart by God. On the other hand, there isn't a single child of God who isn't, in a larger sense, a minister for Him.

It has been said that we are always witnesses whether or not we choose to witness. Good or bad, our lives stand before the world as examples.

We think of ministers as men and women who preach and pray. How often do we think of them as people who do God's pleasure?

Are you receiving His blessings by doing His pleasure?

May I both minister and be ministered to daily, God.

Bless the Lord, all His works, in all places of His dominion. —PS. 103:22

The familiar and well-loved hymn, "All Creatures of our God and King," is attributed largely to St. Francis of Assisi, who loved peace and God's creation. Years later William H. Draper translated it. Some of the phrases reflect Psalm 103:22, beautifully, such as burning sun and silver moon. All join together in praise to God, the Creator, ruler of all. Nature praises God through fulfilling what it has been created to do.

A good example is the sunflower that thrives in hot climates and lifts its face toward God. Another is the chuckling stream that endlessly flows in happy praise, down to a river that in turn leads to lakes and seas.

How long has it been since you slowed down enough to appreciate how God's creation blesses Him, and thus you? Open your eyes today and you will find at least one such blessing.

The blessing of nature brings peace to troubled spirits.

March

BLESSING
BLOCKERS

Jesus said to him, "Thomas, because you have seen Me, you have believed. Blessed are those who have not seen and yet have believed."

—JOHN 20:29

Have you ever had some attitude, belief or feeling hold you back from a blessing? For Thomas, it was the need to see and touch everything firsthand. Even though the other disciples had already seen the Lord, and shared that fact with Thomas, he wouldn't believe it—not until he could touch Jesus himself.

Can you imagine what joy Thomas *missed* by not rejoicing with the others. While they celebrated, he must have fought to hold on to his stubborn insistence that the "impossible" couldn't have happened, especially because he didn't see it.

Doubt isn't all that blocks blessings sent our way. Numerous other human traits are also potential "Blessing blockers."

The stormy month of March is a good time to examine these blessing blockers. And although some of them may not be immediately applicable to you, they may be at some point. By the end of the month, our prayer is that you will be well armed so you may be better able to defeat those attitudes and actions that may rob you of experiencing God's most precious blessings.

Each day this month, O Lord, I desire to overcome a new blessing blocker, beginning with doubt.

"He who finds his life will lose it, and he who loses his life for My sake will find it."

—MATT. 10:39

I'll admit it." Ed confessed. "I have trouble believing that God really does have my best in mind. And I know where this struggle comes from."

Ed went on to tell about his childhood, where nothing was certain. His goal as a youth was to stay away from home as much as possible to escape the terrible effects of all the booze his father drank. Even Christmas wasn't a day of peace. Finally, all the anger and uncertainty he grew up with began to affect him.

Ed's problem is a common one. Unkept promises followed by remorse set a pattern into impressionable young minds that can carry over into adult life. Often what happened all those years ago generates a genuine lack of ability to trust even God!

Today's scripture offers real hope. If you, like Ed, find it hard to develop trust, ask your Heavenly Father to increase your trust in Him. We can lose our lives in Him and find the kind of life we long for when we confess our lack and ask Him to fill the gap.

You are trustworthy, Lord; may I receive Your gifts now.

> *"But I say to you that whoever is angry with his brother without a cause shall be in danger of the judgment."*
> —MATT. 5:22

Unresolved anger is not only an efficient blessing blocker, it can also cause physical, emotional, mental, and spiritual sickness. Psychiatrists, Christian counselors, ministers, and medical doctors regularly see the result of long-held anger. Anger is a killer.

For Christians, the problem often isn't getting angry, but clinging to the extenuating circumstance clause. *Just because* offers an excuse for justifying ourselves. One woman who struggled with a family member's alcoholism came to terms with it once she recognized she'd been angry with him most of her life! The blessing of forgiveness came in a flood but not until she understood "just because" is not a just cause.

Is anger blocking your blessings?

God, please help me to release my anger and know Your blessing of forgiveness.

Pride goes before destruction, and a haughty spirit before a fall.
—PROV. 16:18

This proverb is often misquoted, "Pride goes before a fall." The original quote is far more serious. Pride really does go before destruction.

God wants us to have pride in ourselves, to appreciate what and who we are, for He has given all talents. Self-centered pride, on the other hand, can create havoc and lead to destruction of the family unit. An example is the story of Jim.*

At nineteen, his father ordered him out of the home when Jim wouldn't enter the ministry. Jim's father was a minister who couldn't stand to have three generations of ministers end when Jim couldn't follow the tradition as his older brother had. The father would not accept that one of his own sons wanted to go into marketing. So, the minister told Jim to leave until he would admit the sin in his life and repent.

All the rich family blessings Jim had every right to expect ended with his eviction by a stubborn, prideful father.

Do you have a relationship damaged by pride— yours or the other party's? You can ask God to restore that relationship.

_____

God, please forgive my pride and bless me with humility.
**THE BLESSING, Chapter 9*

"But if you had known what this means, 'I desire mercy and not sacrifice,' you would not have condemned the guiltless."
—MATT. 12:7

The Pharisees were always trying to catch the disciples in anything "not quite right" to add to their complaints against Jesus. In this Matthew 12 incident, they self-righteously labeled the disciples as a bunch of Sabbath breakers, picking grain.

Jesus told them that if they had understood His message they wouldn't condemn the guiltless.

Too bad people don't study this chapter more. If they did, the heartbreak found in this letter to a national columnist need not exist.

Ever since I was a little girl, my mother made me feel guilty if I did not do exactly as she wanted. Dozens of times she has said, "You will be sorry when I am in my coffin." I was never a bad girl. I always did everything she requested me to do. . . .

Both my parents are eighty-two. One of these days my mother will die, and I am terrified of what it will do to me.*

God can deal with these situations. He offers freedom from guilt.

When I am right with You, Lord, please help me leave off the guilt.
*THE BLESSING, Chapter 8

> *Jesus . . . said . . . , "Martha, Martha, you are*
> *worried and troubled about many things. But . . .*
> *Mary has chosen that good part, which will not be*
> *taken away from her."* —LUKE 10:40–42

Some people see Martha as a rigid disciplinarian, a self-proclaimed martyr to duty. Some see Mary as lazy and unwilling to work. However, Martha wanted things to be just right for Jesus. Her mistake was not settling for something simpler so she could also enjoy her guest. Mary may have worked just as hard as her industrious sister, but the desire to sit at Jesus' feet overrode all else.

Jesus saw into both hearts and He actually complimented Martha on her meticulousness. Some Bible versions quote Him as saying Martha was careful about many things. Jesus reminded Martha of her need to rise above all those many things and draw close to Him.

Fatigue, deep weariness, is one of the worst things that can befall us. Do you need the blessing of rest?

Lord, I am often guilty of leading an overcrowded life. May I leave the busyness behind and reach for that "good part" You would never take away.

Whoever has no rule over his own spirit is like a
city broken down, without walls.

—PROV. 25:28

If you have traveled in the Southwest, you've probably wondered about the inhabitants of the early cliff dwellings. Little now remains except broken pieces of a civilization that once flourished.

While it is sad to view the remaining shreds of a once-mighty people, it is even sadder to see today destruction of lives shredded by rebellion. Those who rebel often do so because of a lack of self-control.

All of us know families with rebellious children. Many of us go through a period of rebellion while growing up. Sometimes, parents shrug off their kids' rebelliousness with a helpless, "What can I do?" instead of giving the blessing of discipline that children need to experience. In other cases, parents may lock their kids into a too-authoritarian home. Both situations may breed adult rebellion down the road.

Do you see rebellion in those close to you? In yourself? When you feel rebellion rising, call on Christ for help.

———————

Thank You, God, for stilling rebellion within me.

> *Cast your burden on the Lord, and He shall sustain
> you.*
> —PS. 55:22

We've all seen TV programs about the person who
is under such stress at work he, or she, comes home
and kicks the cat or yells at the kids. The stress of work
can put an end to good family relationships.

A high school principal once said, "If I disliked
twenty percent of my job, I'd walk off it tomorrow."

His secretary gasped, "Twenty percent?! That's not
so much."

"Figure it out," he said. "That's one day out of every
week to be miserable."

Thousands of people today are trapped in jobs,
some well-paying, others at existence level, where
they like maybe only five or ten percent of their work.
Family expenses, rising costs of almost everything,
keep Dad and Mom firmly nailed into boxes they hate
but don't believe they can do a thing about.

Work stress not only affects families, it affects our
ability to receive God's blessings. Have you allowed
stress at work to block your blessings?

Lord, help me set my priorities so I have more time for You.

For the leaders of this people cause them to err,
and those who are led by them are destroyed.
—ISA. 9:16

Isn't it ironic that church, the very place we go to draw close to Christ, can sometimes be a source of stress? There are so many programs, activities, issues, agreements, and disagreements it is easy to get caught up in the whirlwind. Often church stress not only divides a congregation, it can effectively block members' closeness to God.

After a disruption in one church, those who departed continued to plague those who remained. Finally, in response to the discussions, a quiet, but respected woman stated, "This is my church and I'm not going to let anybody take it away from me."

When the world nibbles at our faith in God Himself and says, "See? He let you down," we need to repeat this woman's faith in words and actions. "God is my God and I'm not going to let anybody take Him away. Nothing will shake my faith and my trust."

Lord, with this statement I know You will bless me beyond measure.

> *Better is a dry morsel with quietness, than a house*
> *full of feasting with strife.* —PROV. 17:1

Sundays were difficult for the Johnston family. There was bickering over breakfast and quarrelling over who would sit where in the car. They would arrive at church late, in no mood to worship, and afterwards would criticize everything they could think of. Then they wondered why they didn't get anything out of the services.

The Johnstons didn't realize how negative they'd become until a visiting young cousin observed, "You sure aren't very happy around here, are you?" Then Dad and Mom recognized the problem. Gradually, they worked it out. No more late night TV on Saturdays. Everyone got up a half-hour earlier on Sunday morning. The family had time for a prayer circle before leaving the house.

Not all problems were solved, but there were improvements so when serious problems hit they could work through them together.

Family stress blocks blessings God wants us to have. Resentment, envy, and anger are thunderclouds that block the Son's shining into our lives. Ask God today for a healing of your family.

Lord, please show me how to relieve family stress I am responsible for.

*Now when Job's three friends heard of all this
adversity that had come upon him, each one
came. . . . [to] mourn with him, and to comfort
him.*
— JOB 2:11

Do you have a Bildad, Zophar, or an Eliphaz in your
life?

These were the "friends" who came to comfort Job,
but whose accusations and finger-pointing must have
left him muttering, "With friends like you, who needs
enemies?"

A husband and wife lost their home in a fire. Dazed
and bereft, they couldn't believe their ears when a
close Christian friend asked, "Have you turned from
the Lord?"

"What do you mean?" the homeless man demanded.

"Well, the Bible says real Christians won't be
burned, so I was just wondering . . ."

The couple could hardly contain their anger and
hurt.

Friends are wonderful. But don't look to them always to be your comforter. Even our Lord found His
friends asleep when He needed them at Gethsemane.

---

*God, well-meaning friends can't always bless me, but You can
and do.*

> *"By your great wisdom in trade you have increased*
> *your riches, and your heart is lifted up because of*
> *your riches."*
>   —EZEK. 28:5

People who have no ambition have no aim. Like wild arrows from an inept archer, they never reach the target. At the other end of the spectrum are the people who sacrifice everything to achieve a goal. These people often realize, sadly, when they reach their later years that they have lost irretrievable family and spiritual time to things they no longer consider important.

Getting ahead on the job is a mania. Like other manias, it requires devoted slaves. Abraham Lincoln recognized this danger and addressed it in his words:

> *I am not bound to win,*
> *But I am bound to be true.*
> *I am not bound to succeed,*
> *But I am bound to live up to what light*
>   *I have.*
> *I must stand with anybody that stands right;*
> *Stand with him while he is right,*
> *And part with him when he goes wrong.*

Are you willing to part with ambition when it threatens you?

Let not my ambition, O Lord, stand between us.

*I say then: Walk in the Spirit, and you shall not
fulfill the lust of the flesh.* —GAL. 5:16

Lust is a word we don't hear much about these days.
Too bad. We should. With the rise of sexually transmitted disease and increasing out-of-wedlock pregnancies, isn't it time to discuss the difference between love and lust? This difference can be capsulized in one phrase: immoral versus moral. Love as God created it between man and woman is holy. Lust (called love by the media) is not.

Christians fight the same temptations as those who do not follow Jesus. However, they can be well-armed. Paul puts it bluntly. When we walk in the Spirit, we shall not transgress as a result of lust. To turn the passage around, *if* we allow lust to lure us into illicit relationships, we *cannot* walk in the Spirit, for God has no part in chosen wickedness.

You may struggle with lust, or perhaps were a victim of someone's lust. God offers the blessing of purity and freedom from our own and others' sin.

May you find a new beginning and freedom through our Lord Jesus.

> "[A rich man] thought . . . , 'What shall I do, since I
> have no room to store my crops? . . . I will pull
> down my barns and build greater.'"
> —LUKE 12:17, 18

Why did Jesus condemn the rich man with all the crops? The success of his fields certainly showed diligence. We get a picture of someone who is providing for the future, much the way we put finances away toward our eventual retirement.

Could Christ's rebuke have come because of the selfish hoarding? Did the rich man's greed deprive others? Was he guilty of usury or paying low wages?

We don't know. We do know all his crops and goods didn't keep death away a day longer.

Homes where greed is king turn out unblessed children. Remember King Midas? His was a story of a man who wanted everything he touched to turn to gold. Then he changed his child to a golden statue. What a warning!

Greed sets us on the pursuit of a false god who promises good things and betrays us through our weakness.

Lord, please purge me of greed and fill me instead with a desire to share Your blessings.

For we ourselves were also once foolish,
disobedient, deceived, . . . living in malice
and envy.
—TITUS 3:3

Envy is one blessing blocker that can tear a home apart. Think for a moment how you would feel as one of Joseph's brothers. Twelve boys lived in that home, but only one, Joseph, wore the father's coat of many colors.

Jacob loved that one son more than all the others, and he showed off his favoritism by giving Joseph that colorful robe. This made his brothers see only one color: *red.*

Why do you think Jacob would have expressed such obvious favoritism with his children? Could it have been that he grew up in a home where his own father favored the "hunter," Esau, his twin brother?

If you've felt slighted because of unfair favoritism and have felt the envy and hostility it can create, it's time to deal with those feelings. Uncaring favoritism is wrong, but so too is reacting in out-of-control anger, as Joseph's brothers did.

Just as God ministered to Joseph and eventually to his brothers, so can He take away our frustrations, hurts, and pain. Ask God today to remove any malice or anger in your heart.

God, You put a coat-of-many-colors on all Your children whom You love.

> *He who says he is in the light, and hates his*
> *brother, is in darkness until now.*
>   —1 JOHN 2:9

Forgive and forget" has become a cliché, but it still holds truth. Can we truly forgive as long as we remember every gory detail of what happened? One person said of a friend, "He buries the hatchet alright, but he never forgets where it's buried." The statement implies that at the first hint of trouble with a former foe, the man can go to the exact spot where the hatchet lies and resurrect it immediately.

Hatred within homes produces opportunities to forgive and forget perhaps second only to Christ's forgiveness. Perceived hatred is as bad. Many children grow up feeling that one of their parents or a sibling hates them. It may take years to realize the perceived hatred might have been excruciating pain or extreme disappointment rather than hatred. We cannot walk in the light while hatred of anyone stays in our souls. Do you need to forgive—and forget?

Bless me with selective memory, Lord, that I will remember sins no more.

If God is for us, who can be against us?
—ROM. 8:31

I have a good job, a lovely family, a caring husband, a warm and friendly church. God has blessed me over and over. Maybe that's the reason I get depressed. I find myself in a waiting pattern, as if, suddenly, everything I love is going to be taken away. Then I feel guilty and it makes me even more depressed."

Tammy's current story is a sequel from her childhood. Her father went overboard with praise when she excelled and was deathly cold when she failed. Even in her most triumphant moments, Tammy always carried a little depression in anticipation of not doing so well next time. No wonder in her adult life she waited for the balloon to break.

Many of us need to shine truth's searchlight on our past. Only then can we be free to walk confidently into the future. We must be honest with our feelings regarding missing the blessing. It is the important first step toward healing and restoration.*

Lord, I know You love me and stand by me. May I allow that truth to uphold me.

*The Blessing, Chapter 10

Then Agrippa said to Paul, "You almost persuade me to become a Christian."
—ACTS 26:28

One of the saddest stories in the entire Bible is found in this chapter. Paul had been accused by Jewish leaders on trumped-up charges. King Agrippa, intrigued by Paul's story, wanted to hear for himself what this remarkable man had to say.

What an opportunity for Paul to witness! What an even greater opportunity for King Agrippa to accept the teachings of Jesus. Paul told the story of how the Son of the living God brought him to his knees on the road to Damascus.

Paul went on to ask the king if he knew and believed the prophets. Knowing and believing, did Agrippa hesitate, grappling with the truth he'd heard and against what he felt would be his loss of power? Did he count the cost and find it too high? We don't know. We do know he was almost persuaded, but he couldn't release himself from the terrible grip of power.

Neither can many today. If you have let yourself be enslaved by power on the job, at home, or church, pray for the blessing of release.

———

God, please reveal to me the power blocks I am subject to that I might confess them.

"I know your works, that you are neither cold nor hot. . . . Because you are lukewarm, . . . I will vomit you out of My mouth." —REV. 3:15, 16

Apathy is a growing disease in America today, especially among Christians. For example, a majority of Americans surveyed profess belief in God, yet empty pews across the country show that their belief isn't strong enough to require action.

There is more chance of someone who actively opposes God one day becoming a disciple than of one who has an I-don't-care attitude. At least an adversary is thinking about Him, if only to store up ammunition to use in the fight. Lukewarm people are as insipid as lukewarm chicken broth. No wonder Jesus promises to spit them out.

Lord, I hate lukewarm also; by Your grace I will seek You with more fervor.

> *It is better to trust in the Lord than to put
> confidence in man.* —PS. 118:8

Eleanor's story offers hope. She says, "When I was small, I had little time with Dad. He worked so hard to keep the wolf from the door that our together-time fled out the window. When I was about five, Dad promised he would leave work many miles away to watch me in a church play.

"At the last minute something came up, as usual. I cried and wailed that I wouldn't even be in the program if my daddy couldn't be there.

"My mother finally convinced me that if I let my class down they would feel as disappointed as I was. I did my part flawlessly, but cried myself to sleep afterwards. Hours later I awakened. Dad knelt by my bed, one hand over mine on the cover. I knew he was praying. When he saw I was awake, he hugged me hard and cried.

"'Eleanor.' he said, 'I know you were hurt and disappointed. So was I.' His tears dripped onto my hands. In that moment, all my anger and hurt washed away. He told me people would always disappoint me but God never would."

Heavenly Father, let me feel Your arms around me this day.

*And let us not grow weary while doing good, for in
due season we shall reap if we do not lose heart.*
—GAL. 6:9

Years ago, if you plugged too many electrical items
into an outlet, you blew a fuse. It burned out. If Christians would think of themselves as fuses, perhaps
there would be a decline in burned-out believers.

Dan is an example of Christian burn-out. A fairly
new believer, he vowed never to turn down a chance
to work for his Lord. Keeping that promise led to
teaching a men's class, organizing the monthly business meeting, visiting in homes, and many other activities. At first he reveled in it. Six months later he found
himself resenting the church activities that demanded
all day Sunday, many Saturdays, plus three or four
nights a week. Perhaps he could have continued to
handle the overload if others had accepted and carried
out the programs he worked so hard to implement. But
now, he's joined the stay-at-home group of believers.

It's easy to become weary while doing good, so
keeping our schedules realistic is mandatory, not op-
tional.

*Over-extending ourselves leaves little time for You, Lord, and screens
our awareness of the blessings You extend.*

> *When I consider Your heavens, . . . which You have*
> *ordained, what is man that You are mindful of him,*
> *and the son of man that You visit him?*
> —PS. 8:3, 4

Donald and Mike are in similar businesses. Donald is forceful, successful, and confident. Mike has always struggled in his business relationships.

We can trace the difference back almost to their childhood. Donald's parents praised his efforts. Scrawled pictures and ragged cut-outs adorned the family refrigerator. When he failed at something, his parents reminded him how good he was at other things and encouraged him to try again. They never told him he couldn't do something. He developed high self-worth.

Mike's I.Q. actually tested out higher than Donald's. Given the same affirmation, his self-worth might have been right up there with his friend's. The major reason it didn't happen was the difference in the homes. Mike's parents didn't want "all that clutter" to mar the perfection of their home. "Dummy" was the usual response to something tried and failed.

Mike has struggled with his confidence at work and seeking his confidence in Christ. Yet, with God's love, he can find the genuine worth and acceptance and success he's missing.

Thank You, Lord, that I can find my worth in Your sacrifice for me.

But when the young man heard . . .[Jesus' words],
he went away sorrowful, for he had great
possessions.   —MATT. 19:22

Prestige is first cousin to power and wealth when it comes to being a blessing blocker. Consider the rich young man who came to Jesus asking what good thing he should do to have eternal life.

First Jesus quizzed him concerning his moral life and the keeping of the commandments. The young man had apparently lived an exemplary life. The problem hit when Jesus told him to sell off everything and give the proceeds to the poor. Only then would he have treasure in heaven.

This was not what the young man had expected, or wanted, to hear. From his prestigious position, he could accomplish great things for the Master. What good would disposing of his wealth and becoming just another follower of Jesus do?

Have you ever clung to a high-profile position when the Lord had a more humble job He needed done—one that would bring no honor or recognition? Treasure in heaven is for those who step back from prestige and choose heaven's blessings.

It is sometimes hard to accept Your will, Lord. Help me to choose wisely.

> *"It is easier for a camel to go through the eye of a
> needle than for a rich man to enter the kingdom
> of God."*
> —MARK 10:25

Success stacks right up alongside prestige as a blessing blocker. As children, we try to imagine a real camel going through a real needle's eye. It just won't happen, not even a darning needle.

As adults, we learn that the eye of the needle is a gate in the city walls. In order for a camel to enter, it had to kneel, for the gate was low. Even on its knees, the camel had a tough time making it through—due to the heavy burdens of goods and treasures piled on its back.

Similarly, even when we are on our knees in prayer, if we are occupied with our successes and treasures, how can we fit into the narrow way leading to righteousness and God's blessings? Christians need to separate themselves from the world's false values that say, "Second best is second rate." Not until the final well-done-thou-good-and-faithful-servant awards are given out will we know who is really successful.

Award me the blessing of discerning real success, please, Lord.

"Pray for those who spitefully use you and persecute you."
—MATT. 5:44

A corporate manager ruled his employees with an iron hand. One young man found that every time he had to report to this person, he got sweaty and his head ached. He also discovered that he feared his manager's scorn, so much so that it was eroding his close relationship with God. He almost considered his boss an enemy.

Finally, the employee began to pray for the man and for himself. Months passed without visible sign of change in the boss. However, the blessings the employee received allowed him to relax in his boss's presence and to maintain his dignity and self-worth in the face of scorn.

Without ever knowing why, the boss also relaxed and eventually invited the young man on a fishing trip that established a comfortable working relationship. If someone's scorn is blocking you from God, ask Him to help you deal with it effectively.

God, bless those who spitefully use me. Bless me to Your service.

> *"The Lord does not see as man sees; for man looks at the outward appearance, but the Lord looks at the heart."*
>
> —1 SAM. 16:7

The number of men, women and children who have been abused by family members is phenomenal. Professionals believe only the tip of the iceberg is represented by those now speaking out. Shame, feelings that "it was my fault," and fear of alienating families keep many silent.

A young woman who, after her father's death, disclosed to her family the continuing abuse that had begun at age eight, found herself in a terrible situation. No one believed her. "Why bring it up now, even if it happened?" they demanded. "Besides, if it did, you're the one who let it happen, aren't you?"

Heartbroken, this young woman crawled into a hard shell. It took the special man God sent her plus years of counseling to help her overcome the trauma of abuse and alienation.

———————

Lord, teach me to see on the inside, even as You see, and to be sensitive.

For He Himself has said, "I will never leave you nor forsake you."   —HEB. 13:5

Television periodically airs dramas and news about parents or other relatives who, for one reason or another, abandon children. Sometimes the child is placed in a new home. Others are put into foster care or institutions.

When these forsaken children are interviewed as adults, they typically admit to deep-rooted feelings of worthlessness. Why else would they have been abandoned under even the worst circumstances? Children of divorced parents often feel similarly forsaken, no matter how carefully the situation is explained.

Many of these children grow up experiencing only part of the blessing. They have the consistency of one parent's blessing and the longing for the missing blessing of the other. When the flood of initial attention slows to once a month or less, anger, insecurity, and misbehavior often result.*

God speaks to forsaken children just as clearly as he spoke to all believers. His promise never to leave nor forsake us is sure.

Thank You, Father, for Your everlasting presence, God of all faithfulness.

*The Blessing, Chapter 9

> *"Look at the birds of the air, for they neither sow
> nor reap nor gather into barns; yet your heavenly
> Father feeds them. Are you not of more value than
> they?"*
>
> —MATT. 6:26

Many Christian songs are loosely based on this scripture. Consider the words of "My Times Are in Thy Hand," written by William Freeman Lloyd, 1791–1853.

> *"My times are in thy hand!"*
> *My God, I wish them there;*
> *My life, my friends, my soul I leave*
> *Entirely to thy care.*
> *"My times are in thy hand,"*
> *Whatever they may be,*
> *If pleasing, painful, dark or bright,*
> *As best may seem to thee.*
> *"My times are in thy hand!"*
> *Why should I doubt or fear?*
> *My Father's hand will never cause*
> *His child a needless tear.*

What a marvelous statement of faith and confidence of one who obviously tested God and found Him true.

There are some key words in this hymn that contrast sharply with fear of the future that often blocks off God's blessings. Despite past troubles, we need to trust God from the depths of our soul.

May I, too, know Your hand over me, uplifting, comforting.

For God has not given us a spirit of fear, but of
power and of love and of sound mind.
—2 TIM. 1:7

One of the greatest killers of senior adults in America today is their feeling of no longer being wanted or needed. Believing they can no longer contribute in a meaningful way puts creases in their souls far deeper than the wrinkles in their faces.

Are you facing or living what many call "the golden years"? Do you wonder whether you really make a difference? There is something you can do for God and others no matter what your living situation, age, or physical health.

A story is told of how Mother Teresa enlisted the help of the terminally ill and dying to pray for others. Some of those who committed to praying so lost themselves in concern for strangers they forgot their own problems and, in some cases, got well.

God, I know I am of high value to You. Help me feel this, today.

> *"They all shall know Me, from the least of them to*
> *the greatest of them, says the Lord. For I will*
> *forgive their iniquity, and their sin I will remember*
> *no more."*
> —JER. 31:34

A nurse and doctor stepped outside the room of a critically ill patient. The nurse asked, "How can that broken piece of humanity continue to live? I've never seen anyone so badly hurt."

"Nurse, I honestly believe that man has lived such a wicked life his fear of dying is so great he *can't* die!" the doctor replied.

Thousands experience the same fear to some degree. When confronted with the righteousness of Christ, they can't accept that anyone who had done what they've done could ever be forgiven. This fear is a real obstacle to the healing they cry out for.

Is there something in your life, perhaps carried over from childhood or teen years, that is haunting you and hindering your ability to receive God's forgiveness and your own? Cling to the promise of a God who remembers forgiven sin no more.

I claim the blessing of forgiveness through Jesus Christ, my Lord.

*"For My thoughts are not your thoughts, nor are
your ways My ways," says the Lord.*

—ISA. 55:8

A poem titled "The Hound of Heaven" dramatically portrays someone who tried to run away from God, who pursued him through the years. In reading it, you sense that the one pursued was afraid of what would happen if he allowed God to overtake him.

He isn't the only one. Have you ever heard, "I haven't yet committed myself totally to His will; I'm afraid of what it might be." Or, "I have my life planned. What if God doesn't give me what I've longed for?"

It's really sad when we're afraid to let go of ourselves for fear God will give us the "wrong" blessing!

If ever anyone felt he'd indeed received the wrong blessing, it was Esau (see Gen. 27). Jacob and their mother had connived for Jacob to receive Isaac's blessing to the firstborn. In Esau's misery, he cried out for his father to bless him too.

If a family member has taken the blessing you feel should be yours, take heart. God has reserved the "right" blessing for you.

Father, may I rejoice at receiving the blessing You have for me.

April

ATTENTION: GOD AT WORK

O LORD, You have searched me and known me.
—PS. 139:1

Few things attract attention from passersby more than a large sign marked, **MEN AT WORK.** Christians need to understand and look for the signs marked, **ATTENTION: GOD AT WORK.** Even as the 139th Psalm lists the life areas in which God blesses us, so does the 139th Psalm remind us that God is at work in all aspects of life.

This month we will concentrate on the 139th Psalm and relate it to our lives. Such stories sink into our souls, waiting until we face similar happenings. Then, they can give us courage to continue waiting for God's will.

David's prayer "O LORD, you have searched me and known me" is actually a blessing we can claim. The God who loves us so deeply is the same One who knows us intimately.

How great is our God who searches, knows, and blesses us!

> *You know my sitting down and my rising up.*
> —PS. 139:2

A little girl, counting her Sunday school money, asked her father, "Does God know I'm going to put two nickels in the offering?"

"God knows everything," the father replied.

The girl added another nickel to her offering and whispered, "Guess what, Dad. I'm going to put in *three* nickels and fool Him."

Even though April 1 has been designated April Fool's Day, a lot of people try, *every* day, to fool God.

David's words cut through such subterfuge. Our God, who knows our every move, simply isn't going to be fooled.

Actually, there is great comfort in this. A parallel is found in the awareness a mother has for a small child. Mothers whose deep and abiding love flows in strong currents are mothers who keep close track of their children.

God of love, bless me with the awareness of how much You cherish me.

You understand my thought afar off.
—PS. 139:2

Sometimes I wish God *didn't* know what I was thinking," a teenager confessed to his pastor. "I try to keep my mind clean, but a lot of junk keeps cluttering my brain cells—stuff I don't want God to know about. What do I do?"

"I understand your struggle," his pastor responded gently. "And when I'm trying to clear my head of the junk, I remember Luther's saying: 'I can't stop birds from lighting on my head, but I can prevent them from building a nest in my hair.'"

The teen laughed and then vowed that when the next bad thoughts crept into his mind, he'd drive them out by concentrating on something acceptable.

Have you ever asked God why He didn't change your life? Or (and this is more likely), change the life of someone else who was causing you grief? Such a prayer is often followed by a rush of guilt. It shouldn't be. God understands our thoughts. He also recognizes the basis of those thoughts. Some of His best work is in stilling our anguish and blessing us with peace.

You know my thoughts, Lord. Please speak peace to my heart.

> *You comprehend my path and my lying down.*
> —PS. 139:3

One of the hardest things in life is to round a bend finally and find another major crossroad.

"Not again," we may complain. "Lord, every time I start to feel comfortable, I come on another bunch of decisions. How am I supposed to know which one is the right one?"

Quite often, you won't until you've taken a few steps to test it out.

Derrick and Anthony were husbands who insisted on handling the family finances and major decisions. When Anthony died, Derrick saw how helpless Anthony's wife was managing many of the family's needs. Derrick immediately began teaching his wife everything she'd need to know to survive, so she wouldn't ever be a bewildered widow.

There is great comfort in just knowing You comprehend my path, Lord.

[You] are acquainted with all my ways.
—PS. 139:3

Have you ever observed how husbands and wives grow in resemblance to one another? One reason for this is because each has learned the special ways of the other, those little things that make everyone unique and individual.

God is acquainted with all our ways, and He uses that knowledge to help us become more like Him.

Think of a radiant Christian you know. Close your eyes and picture the steady gaze that looks straight at the world, ignoring the mean and ugly, seeing the beauty. Recall that person's voice. Remember how this saint touches lives. Then, picture the face of Christ. Chances are, you'll see some resemblance.

"It's just his way," we often say of someone. How grand it would be if those around us would remark, "It's *His* way. God's at work in this life."

You aren't finished with me, God. Thank You for the blessing of Your work.

For there is not a word on my tongue, but behold,
O Lord, You know it altogether. —PS. 139:4

According to history, when Charles Wesley accepted the Lord, he told a friend of his experience. He asked the friend if he should treasure it in his heart or if he should tell others.

The advice this friend supposedly gave Charles was that if he had a thousand tongues, he should use every one of them to tell about Jesus.

Charles Wesley wrote over 6,000 hymns. The man nicknamed the "Hymn Writer of the Ages" did use his tongue to praise God. It was the finest work to which his tongue could be given.

Other Scripture warns about *mis*-use of our tongues and warns of the scars this instrument can inflict. Laura remembers hiding in the closet with coats over her head to shut out the sound of her parents' vicious fighting. Mindy remembers her parents' voices raised in prayer. What a different heritage these women carry!

God, bless my tongue and voice that they may be used for You.

You have hedged me behind and before.
—PS. 139:5

Have you wandered through a maze—a living hedge of trimmed shrubs or bushes or trees that has one way in and one way out? A favorite ploy of movie directors is to include a maze for the hero or heroine to use for safety. However, the maze can also increase the potential danger, unless the person knows how to get out. Hedges can both shut in and keep out good and evil.

What does David mean when he says God has hedged him both behind and before? We know this psalm is one of praise and gladness, so it's safe to assume David is viewing God's hedges as protection against unseen snares.

Some families, however, hedge members in by rigid standards to which each person must conform or not feel accepted. Robin's demanding parents almost tore her apart. To please her father, she spent long hours at a job. Satisfying her mother's expectations meant Robin was to do everything for her children her mother had done for Robin, although her mother hadn't worked outside the home. Robin couldn't keep up the pace and eventually her emotional life shattered.* Are there hedges about you? Are they God's hedges or others'?

God's hedges bless us with both protection and freedom to grow.
*The Blessing, Chapter 8

> *[You] laid Your hand upon me.*
> —PS. 139:5

 W hy is the old saying "a helping hand" so significant? Why not "helping feet" or "helping arms"? Perhaps it all goes back to the Old Testament concept of touch. What does the taking of another's hand imply?

Joining hands carries an assurance of warmth, love, trust, healing, and kindness. Every time hands are joined in friendship or love, a blessing is given, a blessing is received. Ralph Waldo Emerson captured the elusive meaning of hand-in-hand with, "I hate the giving of the hand unless the whole body accompanies it."

His meaning is clear when you experience limp handshakes or shifting gazes. It becomes clear that what we want from human touch is more than flesh meeting flesh.

God's hand laid on David is the same hand laid on us. It brings far more than human touch and heals what we may have missed.

God, let me feel Your hand upon me, now and always.

Such knowledge is too wonderful for me; it is high,
I cannot attain it.
                                                    —PS. 139:6

I don't believe in a personal God," Roger would comment. "But the human body is so complex, I often wonder how life began."

An M.D. and Ph.D., Roger knew the intricate workings of the human body. He was studying the genetic make-up of cells in a major cancer center, trying to find a cure for a type of cancer. He was also fighting an inner battle.

Roger called himself a "theistic evolutionist." He had come to believe that a God had to initiate life and creation. After that, the world "evolved." Yet, with every discovery, Roger wondered, *How could anything so incredibly complex just "happen"?*

All of Roger's scientific training and education attributed life to chance and billions of years of development. But Roger began to feel that it took more faith to believe in life by chance than in life created by a mighty force, maybe even God.

Today, Roger is a committed Christian. His knowledge finally proved that life is "too wonderful . . . high" to deny the existence of a living, mighty God.

Thank You, Lord, that even the wisest are humbled by Your wisdom.

> *Where can I go from Your Spirit? Or where can I
> flee from Your presence?* —PS. 139:7

A young boy took small blocks and built a miniature town in the corner of his playroom. Hospital, stores, houses, parks, and a swimming pool. His untrained fingers couldn't quite manage to make roofs so the village lay open to his view.

The boy, on his knees above the town, could see into every corner. No hiding places for tiny toy people existed.

"God is just like this," his mother told him. "There is no place we can ever go where He cannot see us."

What a comfort for those who face painful memories and fears.

While at times we may not feel His presence, He's there. God's Spirit works within us, even in our most desolate hours. God's presence hovers beside us at work, at home, while we sleep. Even when we can't feel Him, we can know He's there.

Bless us with the strength to cling, even when we can't feel Your Spirit, Lord.

If I ascend into heaven, . . . if I make my bed in
hell, behold, You are there.   —PS. 139:8

I've never seen hell but, if it's more miserable than my childhood, I'll do anything to keep from going there," Nanci said in a counseling session. How much easier life would have been, if only this person had known Jesus as a child.

David, in this psalm, is evidently doing a lot of reflecting. He is trying to understand the nature of God. All he can do is to stand and marvel. In this same way, we marvel at how God takes people from hurtful situations, heals them, and leads them into high places to serve him.

My (John's) friend Bull Bramlett is a good example. A former pro football player, he was known as the "meanest man in football" when he played. An angry alcoholic, he also lived in the self-imposed "hell" of anger and addiction. What freed him?

One day, his son's teacher gave him a letter his son had written at school. In a little boy's handwriting were the words that changed his father's life forever, "Lord, please help Daddy not to get drunk this Christmas." God did, and their whole family has been blessed ever since.

Just knowing Your presence is in and through all is my hope, Lord.

> *If I take the wings of the morning, [You are there].*
> —PS. 139:9

Jill's first flight was an early-morning, cross-country trip. Her heart thumped loudly as she took her window seat. Jill braced for takeoff as they lifted into the damp, fresh April air.

Jill looked out the window and relaxed. How different the world looked from on high. She peered out, up, down—and marveled. A whole new world had opened to her, on the wings of morning. Jill felt for the first time the hidden significance of the passage.

David had no commercial airliner in which to experience the sensations that filled Jill with awe. Why did he choose this wording to express himself? Perhaps he had seen cloud formations that resembled wings in the early dawn. Or he may have been thinking of angel wings, bearing him closer to God. We don't know. We can only surmise that, again, he wanted to show the almighty character of God.

Lord, bear me up on the wings of the morning when I am discouraged and need hope.

If I . . . dwell in the uttermost parts of the sea, [You are there].
—PS. 139:9

A ferry boat steadily plowed through the night on its run between Port Hardy and Prince Rupert, British Columbia. In a tiny cabin, deep inside the ship, a sleepless girl lay in her bunk, asking God for release from a gripping fear. If the girl chanced to doze, she came sharply awake with every change in the engine noise and wondered why they had ever decided to include the extra jaunt in their tour of Vancouver Island. *Why didn't we stay longer in Victoria, then return to the States?* The horror of death beneath the waves assaulted her. *Would God let that happen?*

Morning permitted her escape to the deck and joyous freedom in the sunshine. The rest of the trip to Prince Rupert proved gorgeous. Night and its fears receded.

Have you been to life's uttermost depths? Are you struggling toward the surface even now? God is with you and will lift you clear.

Thank You, God, for Your cradling, lifting hands.

> *Your hand shall lead me, and Your right hand shall hold me.*
> —PS. 139:10

Mountain climbers can relate to the words of the psalmist. How many times have they been led by guides to towering heights with only a crumbling ledge or a few footholds made by intrepid climbers who have gone before?

Climbers know their lives depend on their partners. An ignorant guide can spell disaster. An untrained friend can mean the difference between life and death in an emergency. The strong, right hand of one who reaches down to lift a fallen climber may look like the hand of God in its promise of help.

You don't have to be a mountain climber to recognize the blessing of being led and held. Each of us encounters a Mt. Everest in our way, at some point in life. However, God is our guide. His right hand will hold us in a close, caring way.

For the strength of Your right hand, I give thanks, dear Lord.

Even the night shall be light about me.
—PS. 139:11

When young Darrell went to spend a night at Grandma's, he did fine until bedtime. He even helped open the sleeper couch into a bed. Then he hesitated, as if wanting to say something.

Instead, Grandma matter-of-factly said, "Now, we'll leave our doors open in case you need us, but you know what? You might need to use the bathroom. There's always a night light in there that will help you see. And we can plug in this little owl light here so you won't stumble if you get up."

Darrell relaxed.

Grandma smiled, knowing that once Darrell fell asleep he probably wouldn't awaken until morning. If he did, the friendly little owl light would be right there for him.

Night can be a fearsome time for adults as well. Unpleasant or difficult memories haunt us in our vulnerable, sleepless hours. Fears, problems, indecisiveness can all keep us awake, looming like dragons in the shadows. Yet God's Spirit will bless us with rest.

As Your child, God, I claim the blessing of rest.

> *Indeed, the darkness shall not hide from You, but the night shines as the day; the darkness and the light are both alike to You.* —PS. 139:12

When early darkness made walking in the late afternoon inconvenient for two women, one of them coaxed her husband into a moonlight walk. When he agreed, she called her across-the-street friend.

Bundled into warm clothes against the nippy weather, the trio walked under a full moon that turned the snowy ground to silver. They didn't talk a lot. They just walked and enjoyed the sight of night turned to day.

Several more times in the winter months, they walked, experiencing a majesty beyond even the brightest and most beautiful day.

Sometimes the darkness in our lives encourages feelings that, perhaps, even God can't penetrate the specter hovering over us. Yet in His sight, the night and the day are alike. His piercing eye and gentle Spirit easily pass through our darkness as if it didn't exist. Then, He pours the light of His love into our darkest moments.

Help me to seek Your light in my darkness, Lord—and find it.

For You formed my inward parts.
—PS. 139:13

With all the hullabaloo about test tube babies, sperm banks, and frozen embryos, the scientific world sometimes forgets who really creates human life. God's miracle, reborn with every new soul, is still God's miracle, no matter how much experimentation has been done or how unusual or different the circumstances may be.

As the chosen vessel to bear God's Son in a manner never again to be duplicated by all the cleverness of humanity, Mary accepted the task. She rejoiced in it and wept bitter tears. Had those tears been stored up all the years between the time Simeon warned her that a sword would pierce her soul until those terrible moments on the cross?

If only the Bible contained a record of Jesus meeting His mother after the resurrection! The depth and height and breadth of her joy must have surpassed anything any mother had experienced when she saw Jesus risen from the dead.

Thank You, Lord, for the blessing of resurrection.

> *I will praise You, for I am fearfully and*
> *wonderfully made.*
> —PS. 139:14

Some time ago, *Reader's Digest* ran a series of "I am" articles dealing with the different parts of the human body. In first person style, each part told how intricate and necessary it is to humanity.

Not only were the articles interesting and well-written, they reminded readers of what David said—that human beings truly *are* amazing creatures. Current experiments and new treatments for illnesses and disease confirm this. All the elements that comprise a person must be balanced as evenly as the earth in order to properly function.

But, why should we be so amazed at the complexity of a human being? God put His best efforts into mankind who would have dominion over animals, plants, and the rest of the earth. God had already looked on His other works and seen that they were good. How much more exquisitely did He form man and woman?

It is good for us to meditate on how fearfully and wonderfully made we really are. When we do, we have more incentive to take the responsibility to keep ourselves healthy through proper diet, exercise and rest.

May I recognize again the blessings You built into me, Lord.

My frame was not hidden from You, when I was made in secret, and skillfully wrought in the lowest parts of the earth. —PS. 139:15

Anyone familiar with industry knows the importance of secrecy. One area where new creations are jealously guarded is the fashion field. Designers work secretly, protecting their ideas until they are ready to be disclosed.

David wrote of God designing and making us in secret. As with designers, much of God's work is kept under cover until the right time for it to be shown to the world. For a moment, think of God's secret work in your own life.

He is working in you right now, secretly preparing you for life eternal with Him. His Holy Spirit is designing a new and better you, one that will fit into His kingdom.

_____

Thank You, God, for the secret work You do in me.

> *In Your book they all were written, the days*
> *fashioned for me, when as yet there were none of*
> *them.*
> —PS. 139:16

Alan *knew* he could play baseball. But he had come from a small high school that had gotten him little attention and no scholarship offers. Now, he was walking on to a major college team.

"You can try out," the college coach told Alan. "But I'm not promising anything."

Alan played his heart out during pre-season. Two-a-day scrimmages; practice games; hours spent shagging balls.

The day arrived for the names of those who had made the team to be posted. Alan rushed to look for his name on the list.

There it was!

Eventually, Alan won a starting position on the team he hadn't had a chance to make.

Alan's baseball future rested on his name being on a list. Before we are born, our names are written on a list—in God's Book. God knows just how we'll fit on His team: He knows how many days we'll live and what we will be doing. Our comfort is that God, who loves us more deeply than we'll ever know, doesn't require that we try out to make the list.

God of all understanding, help me today to make my day count.

How precious also are Your thoughts to me, O God!
How great is the sum of them!   —PS. 139:17

I know what you're thinking," a little girl told her father. "You're thinking how happy I'd be if you took me to get an ice cream cone."

The words of children are precious. This little one "just knew" her father wanted to get her a treat! While her motives could be questioned, her desire to read the thoughts of her father is unquestioned.

David spoke of how precious God's thoughts were to him. This shows the close relationship they enjoyed. If David had not lived that way, he could not have discerned God's thoughts. Today, many people try to discover what the mind of God really dwells on. Yet unless they are close to Him, it is unlikely they will ever know.

Are God's thoughts precious to you? Do you spend time trying to discern them in your life?

Almighty God, Your thoughts are precious to me.

*If I should count them [God's thoughts], they would
be more in number than the sand.*

—PS. 139:18

The first time Jeff saw the Pacific Ocean, the tide was
far out, leaving a gorgeous stretch of sand. He rolled
in it, played in it, threw it in the air, and covered his
feet with it. Then he began slowly pouring sand from
one hand to the other.

"What are you doing?" his amused mother asked.

"Counting—but there's so much of it!"

Although the psalmist referred to God's thoughts as
more in number than the sand, he could also have said
that God's blessings are more numerous than the sand.
"Count your blessings" is always good advice. Sometimes when we do this, we exclaim, "But there are so
many of them!" At other times, we have to practice
looking for them.

However, there is no day so dull, grey, or stormy
that no blessing exists, though you have to search
harder at such times. Troubles often distort our view
and honest seeking may be required to find even one
good thing. On the other hand, in the seeking, you will
also be blessed.

Blessings around, above, below. Help me to recognize them, Lord.

When I awake, I am still with You.
—PS. 139:18

This Scripture brings to mind an image of someone who talked with God the night before, lay down and slept, then awakened and talked with God again. Here is a person who remained in God's presence throughout the night and into the morning hours.

In the Song of Solomon, God's blueprint for courtship and marriage, the Bride of the King gives us a word picture that captures the essence of this verse, the idea that we are to be with God all of the time. As she seeks ways to picture her love for her husband-to-be, she talks about an Old Testament custom. Women in that day would often carry a sachet of perfume around their neck. That way, during the day, and even the first thing when they awoke, they'd smell the beautiful fragrance they carried next to their heart.

"My beloved is to me a pouch of myrrh," she says. And her thoughts of him are like a fragrance that she carries night and day.

What a picture of how we are to treasure and carry God's thoughts, night and day!

Lord, this day I will be still with and before You. Bless me, I pray.

> *Your enemies take Your name in vain.*
> —PS. 139:20

A young man had the habit of using God's name in a manner that didn't qualify as a prayer.

When he began dating a Christian girl, she appreciated this man's better qualities. He never drank, smoked, did drugs, or got involved with women in unsavory ways.

Their friendship grew, and the time came when she quietly said, "Do you realize how often you use God's name in conversation? You are such a wonderful person, but this really bothers me."

David says it is God's enemies who take His name in vain. True, yet many Christians do the same. They make His name a byword. Even worse are the many ways we take His name in vain through our actions. Once we profess to be His, the eyes of the world look our way, critically, skeptically. When we grow sloppy in our service and lifestyle, we join right in with God's enemies who hold Him lightly. Carrying the name of our Lord is no light matter.

Bless me with recognition of the ways I take Your name in vain, Lord, and enable me to overcome.

Do I not hate them, O Lord, who hate You?
—PS. 139:21

Righteous indignation" is one of the most-often used and least understood phrases in Christian terminology. Too often we justify our anger, disgust, and disapproval under the guise of these two words.

Jesus brought a new understanding and enlightenment when He instructed His followers to hate the sin and not the sinner. This wouldn't be so hard if we could just separate the two in our minds. Neither would it be so hard to forgive parents who withheld the blessing if we could understand why this happened.

For years Andrea had felt distant from her father. Then she learned the five elements of blessing: meaningful touch, spoken words, expressing high value, picturing a special future, and an active commitment. Andrea didn't know whether or not she had received the blessing from her dad.

She discussed her question with him and, in one hour, learned more about her father than in the nineteen previous years. She also gained a new compassion and understanding for him.*

Lord, turn my negative feelings into more righteousness and less indignation.

*The Blessing, Chapter 10

> *I count them [those who hate God] my enemies.*
> —PS. 139:22

It may come as a shock to some, but God actually says in today's verse that there are times when we should have "enemies." Our enemies are those who support the things God says He hates. When we stand against those who hate God, even if we are persecuted, we receive a blessing.

We know of one man who was disgusted with the immoral filth that was being carried on the "Phil Donahue" show. In protest, he organized a writing campaign and sent kind but firm letters to the program's sponsors, informing them of the show's content. Many of the sponsors didn't even know what was being shown.

The campaign has cost that program twenty-eight major sponsors!

We have nothing to fear in standing against our enemies, for God. He is waiting to bless us.

Lord, give me the courage to always be loving, but never be accepting of sin.

Search me, O God, and know my heart.
—PS. 139:23

Earlier in life, David would never have been able to pray this invitation for God to search out the darkest corners of his heart. Now, chastened by the Lord until he had become "a man after God's own heart," David opened his life to God's scrutiny.

One of the ways to maintain a clean heart is to find a spiritual mother or father, a mentor. Many success stories result from the caring of one outside person who sees a need and steps in, investing time and love into another's life. With all the single-parent homes, never has the opportunity been greater for sincere and loving Christians to help fill the gap.

William Shakespeare wrote, "We know what we are, but know not what we may be." The comforting thing is that God knows what we may be and is striving with us to help us become our best. So are His children who have accepted their role as good friends, spiritual mothers and fathers, and mentors. Residents of one college town open their homes so each student has "town parents" and a place to go for help in facing temptation while keeping clean hearts.

God, You are truly my Father. Help me recognize the blessing of earthly spiritual fathers, mothers and friends.

> [God,] *Try me, and know my anxieties.*
> —PS. 139:23

Everyone does not grow up in an environment of unconditional acceptance.

Mark struggled with a strong sense of inadequacy. He kept still, for years, when his mother put him and his siblings down. Comments such as, "Nobody's going to date a fat mess like you!" and "You might as well drop geometry now; that's for smart kids," left them doubting their worth.

The insensitive mother who cuddled Mark's son and wisecracked, "How could anyone as dumb and ugly as you have such a good-looking child?" tipped the scales too far.

Mark had had it. "Stop it! That's all I've ever heard from you. It's taken me years to believe I'm not ugly and dumb. Why do you think I haven't been home in so long? I don't ever want you to call me dumb again." The message his mother had received from her mother had prevented her from pasing on the blessing to her son.*

Lord, may I rest in You when I am anxious.
*The Blessing, Chapter 28

[God] if there is any wicked way in me.
—PS. 139:24

Just one twist of the screw would have saved me an hour of frustration and anguish!

I (John) had set aside one Saturday as "yard work" day. The grass was growing rapidly, and having been out of town with my family, my regular mowing was overdue.

I pulled out my mower, yanked on the starter rope and . . . nothing. Nothing happened on that pull or what seemed like the two hundred other pulls I made that hour.

When I finally gave up and took the mower to the shop (after nearly breaking my back and the starter rope!), I discovered all it needed was one little turn of a carburetor screw.

Roarrrrr! It started right up!

I couldn't believe it. Just one small twist threw off my whole day.

In today's verse, David asks God "if there is any wicked way" in him. The Hebrew word for *wicked* suggests that something is twisted or bent. David wanted to make sure that he was not twisting an attitude or action until it became sin. We need to do the same— or our relationships and our days will be thrown off.

Lord, help me to keep my life strait and pure before You.

> *[God] lead me in the way everlasting.*
> —PS. 139:24

You're lost in a big city where you've never been before. Your feet are tired, and you've given up asking for directions. Either people don't know your hotel or they don't seem to care about your plight.

At a time like that, would you rather come across a city map or find a personal guide who would take you *right* to your hotel?

Anyone would opt for the guide! Maps are great, but a person to lead us is infinitely more comforting.

In the verse above, David asks for a personal guide—God—to help him stay on the right path. As we end our look at this powerful psalm and our fourth month of focusing on God's blessings, perhaps this should be our prayer as well—for personal guidance and to be more like God each day. God loves to answer that type of prayer. And believe me, there's no better Guide in this world, or in the world to come!

Thank You, Lord, for being always willing to be our guide.

May

HIDDEN BLESSINGS

> *"For I will restore health to you and heal you of*
> *your wounds," says the Lord.* —JER. 30:17

Have you ever felt that people couldn't understand or relate to the hurt or pain you've experienced? You're not alone.

It's easy for some people to make fun of someone *else's* pain when they've never experienced its searing bite themselves. As one of William Shakespear's characters in King Leer said, *"He laughs at scars, who himself never bore a wound."*

Many of us carry hidden wounds that need healing far more than our physical bodies. This month we'll be talking about the various *secret* ways God works in our lives. Long before professionals recognized the part our emotions, mind, and spirit play in relation to our physical health, God knew. When He told Jeremiah He would restore health and heal wounds, His promise included our total well-being.

Do you have an unmet need in your life? Look to the most qualified physician/therapist—God.

This month, God, open my eyes to Your hidden blessings.

And seeing the multitudes, He went up on a mountain, and when He was seated His disciples came to Him. —MATT. 5:1

Much of Jesus' ministry took place with crowds of people who clamored for healing and for release from all kinds of plagues. Yet at times, He drew apart with His disciples for special teaching and intimate fellowship.

A point of interest here is the comment, "When He was seated His disciples came to Him." Often Jesus stood when He taught, from a hillside, from a boat. This time He sat down and the disciples gathered close around Him.

A Christian creative writing teacher avoids standing to lecture whenever possible. Unless she is using the blackboard, she either sits on the desk or if the classroom can be arranged so, she sits in a circle among her students, adding an element of fellowship to her teaching.

Take a moment from your busy schedule. Travel, mentally, to that time and mountain where the greatest lessons ever given would soon be taught. Picture yourself next to Jesus, leaning against His knee or looking into His eyes. Then remember that feeling all day.

When we draw close to Jesus, His Spirit wraps us with blessing.

Blessed are the poor in spirit, for theirs is the
kingdom of heaven. —MATT. 5:2, 3

It's hard to believe that anyone who is poor could actually purchase a share of something, particularly when it's the Kingdom of God! Yet that's the truth of today's verse.

George is a man we know who defines *wealth*. He owns an extremely successful company, and has a huge house and a cabin that is nearly as big. He also owns a ranch, an orchard, and several "investment" condos in some of the fanciest places in the country.

Sound like he has it all? Not quite.

For years, George threw his weight around at home and at the office like the rich man he was. He poisoned every relationship he had with his wife and four children, and ended up in broken health and wanting desperately the love his money couldn't buy. Without his family to share his homes and wealth, the homes felt as empty and deserted as a desert shack.

It doesn't take power, might, or a huge bank account to gain real estate in God's kingdom. In fact, it takes a "poor" spirit, one that isn't too proud to admit wrong, ask for help, or be willing to serve others.

If we're struggling financially or otherwise today, it may be humbling to admit it. But just remember, "God resists the proud; but He gives His grace to the humble."

God, may I always be reachable and teachable and available to others.

Blessed are those who mourn, for they shall be comforted.   —MATT. 5:4

We can mourn a major loss nearly as much as we do the death of a loved one. We experience the same disbelief, anger, tendency to blame ourselves, questioning God and finally, acceptance that brings healing.

Phil spent years training for a job in which he felt he could serve the Lord. When he broke into the highly competitive field, he faithfully used every opportunity to witness.

Then, a new supervisor, who didn't like Phil's black-and-white approach to sticky situations, dismissed Phil without warning.

"Why, God?" Phil demanded. "I gave up other chances because I knew this would allow me to serve You."

Two years and much stress later, Phil saw why. The company he had so admired so long had let down its standards. Sales went down and the company folded. Meanwhile, God had led Phil into other work and helped him grow.

Lord, rid me of pride, and keep me meek and teachable.

> *Blessed are the meek, for they shall inherit the earth.*
> —MATT. 5:5

A devout Christian said, "You won't believe how hard it was for me to understand this verse. A Bible teacher cleared things up when he explained that *meek* is a misunderstood word today. The former meaning of meek was *teachable*. That makes a lot more sense to me."

In a world filled with assertiveness training courses, we know of an example of "meekness training" at our church, Scottsdale Bible.

Hosting one of the top youth ministries in the entire country, each week, nearly 300 high school and 250 junior high school students gather for discipleship groups. No skits. Some roudy singing. But always an emphasis on being "FAT"—not in calories, but in teachability. A FAT high school disciple is faithful, available, and teachable.

Are you practicing a "low-calorie" way of being FAT? Such a willing, instructive spirit defines "meekness" as God meant it.

Thank You, Lord, for the new things You will bless me with today.

*Blessed are those who hunger and thirst for
righteousness, for they shall be filled.*
—MATT. 5:6

Remember when you first accepted the Lord Jesus
Christ as your Savior? Remember how you eagerly
read the Bible to get clues into the heart of the One
who loved you and redeemed you? It could probably
be said you actually hungered and thirsted for righteousness.

People hunger and thirst for a lot of things these
days: parental and peer approval and acceptance,
money, power, possessions. How many hunger and
thirst for righteousness enough to brave dangers or
obstacles?

If you've had the opportunity to observe wild animals, you know they are usually quite cautious. Con-
trary to popular screen portrayals, cougars and wolves
normally do not attack people. When they do, it is gen-
erally because hunger has driven them far from their
normally well stocked habitat. They pursue satisfac-
tion for their hunger and thirst; they pursue survival.

Have you been pursuing righteousness—survival?
Isn't it time you directed your great desires toward
God?

_____

You have promised that I will be filled, Lord. Thank You.

Blessed are the merciful, for they shall obtain mercy.

                        —MATT. 5:7

When Jesus says the merciful will be blessed, He doesn't say they will be blessed with honor and glory and praise. He never promises that if you are merciful a national magazine will automatically bang on your door, wanting to write your story so the world will be impressed. Most often the greatest acts of mercy remain known only to the giver, the recipient, and God.

What Jesus does promise to the merciful is far better and more lasting than fleeting fame. He vows that those who consider and bear with others will obtain mercy for themselves.

For Your mercies, I rejoice, and for the blessings that fill me when I do Your will.

*Blessed are the pure in heart, for they shall
see God.*
—MATT. 5:8

Our good friend, Chuck Swindoll, told a story we couldn't help laughing at. For nearly two decades, this godly pastor has served up encouraging words to his congregation at First Evangelical Free Church of Fullerton, and to a world-wide audience on his radio program, "Insight for Living."

The day before he and Cynthia came out to Southern California for their first visit to the church, it had rained steadily all day. When their plane landed that next morning, the clouds had left and the skies were blue and washed clean of any smog. When Chuck asked where the haze he expected was, one man who would later become a close friend looked at him with a straight face (and a twinkle in his eye), and said, *"Smog?"*

After he took the pastorate, unfortunately, Chuck saw firsthand one of the few unattractive things about that part of the country—the pollution that obscures the nearby hills.

Jesus talks to us today about inner pollution and how only those whose lives are clean can see God clearly. Like a night of rain, we need to ask God's Spirit to cleanse us of sin each morning. And all throughout, we need to seek to have a pure heart that we might clearly see our Lord.

O God, may I be pure, and may I always seek Your face.

> *Blessed are the peacemakers, for they shall be*
> *called sons of God.*　　　　　　—MATT. 5:9

I never felt like a real son to my father," Clint said. "Sometimes I wondered if he didn't think Mom had brought the wrong child home from the hospital."

Clint, like many children, teens and adults, considered himself a misfit in his family. Isn't it comforting to know that there are no misfits in God's family?

Clint went on to say that a neighbor, Kirk, actually parented him more than his own dad. Kirk attended school concerts when Clint's father was "too busy" for them. He encouraged Clint to develop his musical ability and worked to understand and support this particular boy.

Jesus promises that the peacemakers shall be called the sons of God. Perhaps this is because Jesus came to bring peace to those who accepted Him. Or, perhaps, it's because those who have deep concerns for peace are near to the heart of God.

Bless me with peacemaking skills, Lord; I long to be Your child.

Blessed are those who are persecuted for righteousness' sake, for theirs is the kingdom of heaven.
—MATT. 5:10

It's naive to think that people are no longer persecuted for their Christian beliefs as they were in the past. Story after story of those imprisoned around the world show how strongly Satan is working against the influence of missionaries and Christian workers.

All the persecution isn't limited to faraway places, either. There are people in our own country who have been disowned by parents and friends because they cling to the Lord rather than past lifestyles.

Plutarch wrote, "God is the brave man's hope, and not the coward's excuse." When we feel every hand is against us, we can still have that unquenchable hope.

Have you been ostracized because you stood for the Lord? No one wants to be shunned and ignored, but God promises blessings in the very middle of the persecution! He also promises that the kingdom of heaven will belong to those who face this kind of situation.

I need Your strength, God, to withstand persecution, for righteousness' sake.

> *Blessed are you when they . . . say all kinds of evil*
> *against you falsely for My sake.* —MATT. 5:11

One of the hardest things to overcome is being the subject of lies by some jealous or vindictive person. It's even worse when the gossip not only damages relationships, but casts doubts on your character.

Jesus knew some of His disciples must be concerned about what their associates thought of the wild move they had made in following Him. Not all those in the multitudes who swarmed to hear Him came with friendly feelings or to learn. Scribes and Pharisees came to prove they were right and Jesus was nothing but a charismatic imposter.

We don't know what Andrew and Peter's neighbors had to say, but the Galilean grapevine must have been in perfect working order. It may well have been that even some of the disciples' families said harsh things.

Tomorrow we will see Jesus' amazing answer to cruel gossip.

How marvelous that even as others condemn me, Lord, You bless me.

Rejoice and be exceedingly glad [when you are persecuted], for great is your reward in heaven, for so they persecuted the prophets who were before you.
—MATT. 5:12

The Law and the Prophets meant everything to good, faithful Jews. That's why today's verse would have meant so much to the disciples.

When Jesus admonished them to rejoice and be exceedingly glad when others criticized, gossiped, and lied about them, He linked them with the best. Not only did He promise them a great reward in heaven— a treasure to be cherished and to anticipate—He elevated these humble men from the ordinary to the ranks of their heroes! He put them in a class with revered men who had left indelible marks on history.

Jesus speaks to us today in the same way. We may face scorn and heartbreak, yet we are not alone. Neither do we have to wait for a heavenly recompense. He stands with us in all persecution.

Lord, teach me to rejoice in bearing the same persecution You and the Prophets bore.

"You are the salt of the earth."
—MATT. 5:13

One of the highest compliments we can be paid is, "You are really salt of the earth." This expression has come to stand for all the characteristics we respect, such as endurance, steadiness, and moral uprightness. Often in books, New Englanders are portrayed as the salt of the earth, as are the steadfast pioneers.

If you've ever been on a salt-free diet, you can better appreciate salt. There are lots of substitutes available, but, like Jesus, most of us don't want substitutes. We want salt to flavor our food. Jesus wants Christians to flavor the world.

The exciting thing is that it doesn't take a whole lot of salt to make the difference between bland and tasty. About the time we despair of ever really making a difference, when it feels like there are so few followers compared with the lost, God reminds us that a few, tiny grains of salt can change an inedible concoction into good food. In the same hidden way, Christians change a wicked and indifferent world to one of blessing and caring.

———————

Bless Your people, Lord, that we may never lose our flavor.

*"You are the light of the world. A city that is set on
a hill cannot be hidden."*　　　—MATT. 5:14

The second Sunday of May is designated as Mother's
Day, a day mothers across America are celebrated.

Not all "mothers" have actually borne children.
Many simply possess the qualities of motherhood.

True mothers' lives are lighted with an inward light,
regardless of their circumstances. One such woman,
Harriet Tubman, risked her hard-won freedom and her
life to bring hundreds of people from the darkness of
slavery into the light of God's freedom. Harriet Tubman escaped slavery via the underground railroad to
Philadelphia then returned south, again and again, to
help others. She held high the torch of her belief and
never let it be extinguished or stopped reaching out to
care for others, even when a $40,000 reward was of-
fered for her capture.

We need to light up our world, even if it costs us.

Lord, please show me how to light my corner of the world, for You.

> *"Let your light so shine before men, that they may see your good works and glorify your Father in heaven."*
> —MATT. 5:16

Have your ever been camping, far away from any city lights? It's amazing how dark it can become outside your campfire, and how quickly!

The next time you go camping, (even if it's only in your backyard), try an experiment. After sitting next to your fire, stand up and begin walking away from the campfire. With every step you take, you feel as if you are being swallowed up in darkness. And just feel the relief when you turn back towards the fire and walk back to camp.

Several years ago, a group of miners were trapped in a cave-in. Buried deep underground, they were finally rescued by the heroic efforts of those above. What was the one thing they longed to see, and the very thing they were most thankful for when it happened? A beam of light shining down from a rescuer's flashlight.

Spiritually, it doesn't take a huge spotlight to draw attention to how great our God is. All it takes is for one, committed person to so let his light shine before men, that a world lost in darkness welcomes the light.

Today, hold high the torch of your love for Christ. It can change your life and the lives of others.

What can I do today, O Lord, to let my light shine brighter?

*"Give to him who asks you, and from him who
wants to borrow from you do not turn away."*
—MATT. 5:42

This is a tough verse to understand, yet Jesus may not have limited His thoughts simply to finances. He had no money or riches. The treasurer of His little group carried the purse and undoubtedly purchased their food.

The opposite side of the picture is that we don't read of Jesus withholding what He did possess—His concern, healing, compassion, love, and virtue.

The person who first observed that it was better to give a man a fishing pole than a fish, typifies the giving of far more than a bandage to cover a cancer.

Does Jesus mean we should indiscriminately give everything we have to those who won't work or who take advantage of friendship? Certainly not. But He does want us to learn the joy of sharing and the freedom that comes from not being so possessive we cannot help those in need.

Bless me with Your giving Spirit and with discernment to know how best to pass on blessings.

> *"Therefore you shall be perfect, just as your Father in heaven is perfect."*
> —MATT. 5:48

The very idea of being perfect is enough to scare some of us out of our shoes. Many have already experienced the rejection and withholding of the blessing by parents who demanded perfection making us feel as if we'd never measure up.

But Jesus never gave an impossible commandment. When He said we are to be perfect, He meant it. However, His definition of *perfect* differs from ours. In Greek, the word *perfect* meant "maturity."

Jesus Himself was perfect. He was also the son of a carpenter. He must have spent hours in the carpenter shop. Did He never misjudge the length of a board? Was every nail He drove, even as a child, arrow-straight and to the mark?

Maturity is a process, not an all-at-once achievement. As long as we are striving each day to come closer to Him and to know His will, His blessings are working in us so that we can be perfect in His sight.

Thank You, Lord, for the blessing of Your example.

When you [give, do so in secret] . . . ; and your
Father who sees in secret will Himself reward
you openly.
—MATT. 6:3, 4

It is our joy to know of a man who is a "secret" giver. The owner of a major corporation, he has personal assets and a personal trust fund that disperse gifts to ministries and individuals—with one catch. Like the old television show "The Millionaire," the person receiving the gift must not know the source of the gift. Our friend sends the gift through a pastor or trusted friend who is not at liberty to disclose his name.

Our friend takes today's verse very seriously. He knows that he has been financially blessed by God in his business. But he also knows that, unlike those "religious leaders" in Christ's day who paraded their gifts before men, he is not to do that.

It's natural to want to be recognized for doing good. But Jesus tells us that recognition is never to be our primary goal. Doing good for others should come out of an overflowing life that doesn't look to other's praise for fulfillment. For when we're filled to overflowing with God's spirit and love, we're really free to give, no strings attached.

Lord, don't let me miss an opportunity to help others so I can build Your kingdom, not my pride.

> *"Judge not, that you be not judged. For . . . you will*
> *be judged . . . with the measure you use."*
> —MATT. 7:1, 2

Every day we are judges. Most of us aren't wearing black robes, but we are called on to make judgments each day. We judge the merits of one school over another, one brand of soap or vegetable or box of cereal as compared with all the rest on the shelf.

Jesus isn't addressing the choice judgment but the hard core judging of other human beings when he warns that the way we treat others is what will come back to us.

A sad thing is that we often make snap judgments based on dislike of the way someone walks or wears her hair. First impressions may be reliable, but in many cases they are not, and the damage is done when we make a judgment without knowing anything about the other person.

Help me to rethink a negative judgment I've made and bless me with the grace to make amends, Lord.

Whatever things are true, . . . meditate on these things.
                              —PHIL. 4:8

Every verse in the Bible is important, but some contain the essence of life itself. This is one of them. Paul is specific about that on which we should concentrate.

For the next several days, we will discuss the elements of this verse and explore how they can enrich our busy lives.

Whatever things are true may have been easier to discern in Paul's time. Today, we are bombarded with thousands of truth-claims. Yet if we are to recognize God's blessings, especially His hidden ones, we must take time to reflect and separate the imitation from the real.

"Truth is what you make it" may be our world's current version of "wisdom." But don't believe it. Truth is what *God* made it at creation, and it hasn't wavered at all since. We may mince words and twist actions, but keep your eyes on God's Word for truth and life!

Open my understanding, God, and help me see the truth of heaven here and now.

*Whatever things are noble, . . . meditate on
these things*
—PHIL. 4:8

It's been a terribly difficult year for the Royal Family in England. The Queen of England even said so in her Christmas address to her country!

Two divorces, one involving a prince and another a princess, are the first divorces for the immediate family in almost 400 years. Another royal heir remarries for the first time in nearly 70 years, and to top it off, Windsor castle where the Queen lives nearly burns down!

While none of us can understand the pressures and incredible scrutiny that the Royal Family goes through each day, they have seen their "noble" image tarnished this year.

The word, noble, can mean "high birth," or "exalted rank." Yet with such rank comes high expectations as well.

In today's verse, Jesus tells us that those things that are worth the most, are the very things we're to meditate on. And what could be of more worth than our Lord Jesus and His Word.

As children of the King of Kings, we already have a "noble" heritage. May we live up to our high calling as we seek to honor Christ before the world this day!

May I use our noble heritage to bless others.

*Whatever things are just, . . . meditate on
these things.*
—PHIL. 4:8

How long has it been since you repeated the Pledge of Allegiance?

I pledge allegiance to the flag of the United States of America and to the Republic for which it stands, one Nation, under God, indivisible, with liberty and justice for all.

More than a hundred years have passed since this pledge was written by Francis Bellamy, an associate editor of the old *The Youth's Companion* magazine. Is there any more liberty and justice now than back then?

Thankfully, yes! Although not everyone in America receives justice, the turbulent years of war and peace, riots and striving have resulted in many positive steps forward.

As thrilling as it is, no pledge can ever ensure liberty and justice for all of a country's citizens. If you are a victim of injustice, take heart. God's mercy and justice will be yours.

In an unjust world, Lord, bless us with the courage to fight and obtain justice for all, not just for some.

> *Whatever things are true, whatever things are*
> *lovely, . . . meditate on these things*
>
> —PHIL. 4:8

Paul combined his admonition to meditate on things pure with things lovely. Perhaps it is more than chance that caused this sequence? Purity, perhaps, is a prerequisite to loveliness.

Did you ever take home a basket of ripe, lovely peaches, only to discover when you cut them open, rotten peaches.

People who have allowed sin into their hearts may be like the peaches. The most gorgeous face, now and then, hides falseness, although eventually, the real person inside creeps out through the windows of the soul.

A blow to a peach while it is in the formative stages may bruise and begin the rot that may not show up until later. Just so can nurtured sin begin the rotting-away process inside us.

Are you fighting something that threatens to mar your heart and soul? Ask for the blessing of release—today.

_____

Thank You for the purity and loveliness You send, Father.

*Whatever things are of good report, . . . meditate
on these things.* —PHIL. 4:8

Report card time among students can be traumatic
or exhilarating. How does *your* report card look? Are
you passing on the blessing to others, and experiencing the return blessing? On a scale of 1–10, evaluate
yourself on bestowing the blessing.*

1. Do I meaningfully touch?

1	2	3	4	5	6	7	8	9	10
RARELY									FREQUENTLY

2. Do I speak words of blessing?

1	2	3	4	5	6	7	8	9	10
SELDOM									OFTEN

**3. Am I attaching high value to the people I'm
blessing?**

1	2	3	4	5	6	7	8	9	10
LOW VALUE									HIGH VALUE

4. Have I pictured a special future for their life?

1	2	3	4	5	6	7	8	9	10
SELDOM									OFTEN

**5. Overall, my commitment level to fulfill my
words of blessing is:**

1	2	3	4	5	6	7	8	9	10
VERY LOW									VERY HIGH

Help me to daily grow in giving and receiving Your blessings, Lord.
*The Blessing Chapter 7

If there is any virtue . . . meditate on these things.
—PHIL. 4:8

Virtue can be seen as a sister word to worthy. Virtue is that which lifts us from the mire and sets us on the path to becoming worthy.

Have you checked your habits lately? What kind of books do you read, music do you listen to, movies do you watch, conversations do you engage in, thoughts do you have? The answers to these questions should be considered in the light of the question, "How much virtue or worth is present?"

A young woman maintained that it didn't hurt her to read torrid love stories or view X-rated films. Months later she realized that where her attention had been, her thoughts remained. She vowed to no longer participate in or surround herself with anything worthless. If activities and conversations held no virtue, she found others that did.

Bless me with the discrimination to cling to the virtuous, God.

*If there is anything praiseworthy—meditate on
these things.*
—PHIL. 4:8

Are you trying to give the blessing through active
commitment to your children? Becoming a student of
those whom you wish to bless is a great way to begin.

To become a student of your children, it is helpful to
take the initiative in asking questions.*

Do You Know the Following Things about Your Children?

1. What do they dream about most often?

2. What do they think they would like to do as young adults?

3. What person in the Bible would they most like to be like? Why?

4. What do they believe God wants them to do for humankind?

5. What type of friends, boyfriends, girlfriends are they most attracted to? Why?

6. What are the best and worst parts of their school day? Why?

Help me to be praiseworthy, Lord, and to help others be the same.
*The Blessing Chapter 7

> *Therefore take up the whole armor of God, that*
> *you may be able to withstand in the evil day, and*
> *having done all, to stand.* —EPH. 6:13

Another encouraging section of the Bible is Paul's letter to the Ephesians. His picturesque comparisons stir our imaginations.

Paul had seen evil days. He had also been given a vision of the future when things would get worse rather than better. When he speaks of putting on the whole armor of God, he sees people prepared to stand against Satan.

It's interesting to note that Paul advises us to put on the whole armor. Modern soldiers going into battle are cautioned to never remove their helmets. The rationale is that head injuries are more dangerous than other injuries. Paul knows that every part of us needs protection: body, mind, spirit, heart and soul. He gives specific directions on how this can be done, and each is a blessing from our Heavenly Father that arms us against any adversity.

Father, please teach me to put on the armor and stand faithfully for Jesus.

Stand therefore, having girded your waist with truth, having put on the breastplate of righteousness.
—EPH. 6:14

The word *girded* isn't often heard these days except for occasional references to scriptural accounts of soldiers preparing for battle. Webster defines gird as the act of binding with a flexible band or belt. What if every Christian were bound with the flexible band of truth? What if we were held together by undeniable truth and right; surrounded with the power that truth alone can offer?

Down through the ages, wicked people have tried to stamp out the truth of God and His Son, Jesus Christ. They have scoffed and belittled, "proved" God could not be real, crushed and killed believers. The same truths Jesus taught by the Sea of Galilee are as alive and wonderful today, as then.

Another armor piece is also important in battle. It is the breastplate of righteousness. It protects and shields our most vital parts. When we don the breastplate of righteousness, our hearts are armed.

Encompassed by truth, shielded by righteousness, we are blessed with the strength to stand.

*[Stand,] having shod your feet with the preparation
of the gospel of peace.*
                                              —EPH. 6:15

Hundreds of shoe companies offer everything from improved sports ability to comfort and style. Each type of shoe is designed for a specific purpose. You wouldn't wear a pair of even the fluffiest, warmest house slippers to the White House. Sneakers will never replace golf shoes. High heeled pumps won't serve well in the woods.

Paul, too, recommends special shoes. These help the wearer walk the path of life more easily and stand more firmly. Note that he doesn't just say we should be shod with peace. No, our shoes are to be the preparation of the gospel of peace. In other words, knowing and walking in the gospel of Jesus Christ will, eventually, result in everlasting peace.

How many pairs of shoes are in your closet right now? Perhaps you need to trade some in for a pair of Paul's Specials?

May my feet be swift in Your service, my God.

[*Stand*], taking the shield of faith with which you
will be able to quench all the fiery darts of the
wicked one.   —EPH. 6:16

Years ago, what is now celebrated as Memorial Day,
was, in the South, called Decoration Day. Following the
Civil War, southern women began the custom of deco-
rating the graves of those who had died for The Cause.
This was Decoration Day.

Nell reflects, "Decoration Day was a highlight of our
year. We all gathered at the cemetery for a joyous and
faith-renewing time of remembering those the Lord
had taken. Afterwards, we met for a picnic or potluck.
Our children learned to know and love relatives they
had never seen. We taught them how their godly an-
cestors had served the Master. We also taught them
that they would someday get to meet these people, if
they also chose to follow Jesus. Death held no fears
for us and we learned to see it as a temporary separation only."

What a blessing!

Lord, please help us create a strong family heritage in You.

> *Take the helmet of salvation, and the sword of the*
> *Spirit, which is the word of God.* —EPH. 6:17

Here, Paul turns to an offensive weapon, rather than just defensive armor. The sword of the Spirit, or the Word of God, can serve us well.

Many basketball coaches admonish their teams, "The single best defense is a great offense." This may be true in the lives of Christians, as well. Remember the reason why Paul said, in verse 13, we are to take up the whole armor of God? So we could withstand the enemy, standing firm.

Michael knows what withstanding and standing are. He spent time in a POW camp. First, he had to withstand the horrors and indignities inflicted on him. Then he had to stand the loneliness, privation and endless months. He came through the experience a changed man. Michael found that if he repeated Bible verses he'd learned as a child, God blessed him with the ability to endure. The word of God indeed proved to be the sword of the Spirit for him.

Lord, when we are hard pressed, bless us with Your word.

June

THE LORD
BLESS YOU . . .

> *And the LORD spoke to Moses saying: "Speak to*
> *Aaron and his sons, saying, 'This is the way you*
> *shall bless the children of Israel. Say to them:*
> *"The LORD bless you and keep you;*
> *The LORD make His face shine upon you,*
> *And be gracious to you;*
> *The LORD lift up His countenance upon you.*
> *And give you peace."'*
> *"So they shall put My name on the children of*
> *Israel, and I will bless them."* —NUM. 6:22–27

This Scripture passage is rich with meaning—"foundational"—for those of us who want to experience God's blessings. In fact, these verses will provide the overall guidelines for the next six months of devotions!

In this beautiful month of June, it's only fitting that we focus on the very first element of this often quoted blessing, "The Lord bless you."

In the days to come, may you see new ways to believe, feel, and share God's blessing in your life!

Thank You, Father, for taking the initiative in loving me.

> *"In these last days, (God) has spoken to us in His Son."*
> —HEB. 1:2

Think back to those awkward days in junior high. Did you ever have a "crush" on someone but lack the courage or opportunity to tell them of your feelings? It's hard to get up, walk over to someone, and say face-to-face, "I think I like you very much."

The fear of rejection or ridicule can paralyze us. I know of one person whose fear of rejection from his current high school friend caused him to interpret the busy signal on her phone when he called as proof positive that she didn't want to talk with him!

What a different way God has of expressing His love! While those of old had to rely on Judges, Prophets and Kings to tell them *about* God . . . we get to learn firsthand of God through His Son. God actively *seeks* to reveal His love for us, directly through His Son. No clearer revelation could ever be.

Thank You, Lord, for taking the active step to reveal Yourself through Your Son.

> *In these last days [God has] spoken to us by His
> Son, whom He appointed heir of all things.*
> —HEB. 1:2

The charming book *Little Lord Fontleroy* tells the story of an old, crochity English lord who meets his match in his grandson.

In a fit of rage, the bitter old man had sent away his only daughter because she had fallen in love with an American. His daughter chose love over her title, and traveled to the United States. Finally, however, she sent her grandson to meet his grandfather. The boy won his heart and proceeded to reunite his mother and grandfather and regain the inheritance his mother had been denied.

Have you ever received an unexpected inheritance? Whether you realize it or not, you have a claim in a priceless inheritance. As a child of God, you're related to Jesus, the heir of all things! That does not mean He will shower you with earthly riches, but it does mean that you have a share in His spiritual riches and kingdom.

_____

The inheritance of a godly life is what I want to leave others, O Lord.

I will praise You with uprightness of heart.
—PS. 119:7

Uprightness is a word that immediately forms a picture in our minds. Perhaps you have known someone who was upright—perhaps a father-figure. June is the month in which we honor fathers. It can also be a time to remember other men who have helped us fulfill our dreams.

Think back to a pastor or counselor, a favorite teacher or a relative who can only be described as upright. What makes you remember this person? His wealth? Possessions? Personality? Power? It's more likely that he impressed you (and upright adults impress kids and teens more than they may ever realize) because of his firm hold on life and his refusal to lower his morals or standards. God, the Father, delights in such men, women, and children.

May I march forth and praise You, God of our fathers.

> *With my whole heart I have sought You; oh, let me*
> *not wander from Your commandments!*
> —PS. 119:10

Robert Robinson wrote in the last stanza of the hymn "Come Thou Fount of Every Blessing" a heartfelt cry, familiar to Christians of all ages.

> *Prone to wander, Lord, I feel it,*
> *Prone to leave the God I love;*
> *Here's my heart, O take and seal it,*
> *Seal it for thy courts above.*

It is doubtful that any Christian who sings these words cannot identify with them. We love God. We seek Him, as did David. Yet we are prone to wander.

Becky is an example of someone who loves the Lord but finds it difficult to stay close to Him. She feels pressured to dress in more expensive clothing than she can afford. It affects her ability to give freely to others in real need. Often she purchases a garment, wears it a few times, then grows dissatisfied with it and herself. Repentance follows, but always with the knowledge her real problem is wandering from the simple paths she knows are God's.

Lord, do not let me wander from You.

Your word I have hidden in my heart, that I might not sin against You. —PS. 119:11

How satisfying to find an old diary or letter on paper, yellowed and crumbling! To discover writing that may have lain hidden in a trunk for years, forges new links in the chain to the past.

What treasures lie hidden in your attic? What words of life are hidden in your heart?

David specifically stored the Word of God in his heart that he might not sin against God. The Word can be stored in our lives, as well.

A young woman, who must have paid more attention in Sunday school than she remembered, found herself faced with a serious choice between right and wrong. To her amazement, just when she opened her mouth to agree with the one who tempted her, one of the Ten Commandments flashed to mind. It stilled her tongue and changed her life.

Thank You for the treasure of Your Word, Father. May I hide it in my heart so it will be there when I most need it.

> *"Who being the brightness of His glory and the express image of His person."*
> —HEB 1:3

Several years ago, I (John) was staying at a friend's home. I was awestruck at the beauty of the house, inside and out.

In one room, above my friend's grand piano, I noticed a familiar print of a cowboy in winter, by the famed Western artist (and outstanding Christian) G. Harvey.

My wife and I had this same, gorgeous print hanging in our home. So when my friend's wife walked into the room, I couldn't help but remark on their "good taste" in art.

"We have this same print in our house!" I exclaimed. But as I looked at her smile, and then back at the print, I realized I was not looking at a *print*. This was the original oil painting that our print (and several thousand others) had been made from! No *wonder* it looked so beautiful.

We will experience a similar awe when we see our Lord Jesus, who is the exact representation of the Almighty God. What a blessing we will have the day we see the "real thing," face to face.

Thank You, Jesus, that one day we'll get to see Your radiant smile.

I will delight myself in Your statutes; I will not forget Your word. —PS. 119:16

After speaking with a helpful guard, I'd finally found the right panel. From there it was only a matter of going up twelve rows and finding the second name in.

There, carved into the somber black granite wall, was the name of my (John's) good friend, lost during the Vietnam war. He was only twenty when he died. Already a veteran of one tour of duty, he went back for a second tour, only to walk into eternity.

I'll never forget his funeral. His father had already passed away, and his mother was all that was left of his family. Yet, in the sadness of that overcast January afternoon, there was a light in his mother's eyes. An outstanding Christian, she had made only one "special" request of the pastor as he prepared his message: "Please tell them not to forget my son."

While the Vietnam Memorial may help future generations remember my friend's name and sacrifice, I don't need it. His name, face, and smile come back each time I drive past the graveyard where his marker lies or visit the Wall.

I remember my friend's name because it's so valuable to me. And in a similar way, God calls us never to forget His words. The more precious, the more valuable His Word is to us, the less chance we'll ever forget it and the more delight we'll take in it.

Help me remember and cherish Your Word, Lord.

> *Open my eyes, that I may see wondrous things*
> *from Your law.*
> —PS. 119:18

Ernest and Edna had little money to give their children. The Great Depression left them with plenty to eat from their garden, a warm, dry house, clothing made over again and again and only a few dollars for flour and sugar.

Thirty years later, the children firmly maintain they were the richest children alive!

"Dad and Mom took us to the woods, the river, the fields," Gary says. "No tiny insect, flying bird or crumpled leaf escaped Dad's keen attention. He opened our eyes to the wonder of creation."

"Mom always seemed to have just enough ingredients for a batch of cookies," Loraine adds. "And we learned about the wondrous lands far from our own by reading good books."

Our Heavenly Father blesses us by opening our eyes to the wondrous things in His creation and in His laws that rule His creation.

———————

Too long have my eyes been blinded, Lord. Open them to You.

"For to which of the angels did He ever say: . . .
I will be to Him a Father,
And He shall be to Me a Son?

—HEB. 1:5

Nine weeks ago today, my (John's) father died. I only wish the circumstances could have been different. The man whose hand I held and who I prayed for during the last eight hours of his life was more a stranger than a father to me.

My father had left my mother when I was four months old. I wasn't old enough to retain a memory of him then, and I did not meet him again until I was in high school. After that, I saw him only on rare, often negative occasions.

Like many who have grown up in a single-parent home, I know what it's like to have to go to the "Father-Son" banquet with a neighbor's dad or never to have your father at a game or to talk to about important decisions. Because of this, one of the most powerfully compelling aspects for me in the relationship God wants to have with us was the father/son connection.

In today's verse, we see that in contrast to the angels, who could only wish to have such a relationship with God, Jesus shared that father/son bond with the Almighty God. And the wonderful truth is that even if we were orphans in our home, we, too, can share a father/son tie with our Heavenly Father, through Christ. That can give us a sense of completion that can fill all the missing pieces!

Thank You, Lord for filling the loneliness from missing a parent.

> *Your testimonies also are my delight and my*
> *counselors.*
> —PS. 119:24

There are two ways people try to "change" in counseling. The first type of change is called "first order change." First order change involves an effort to change that results in no change at all.

Have you ever had a nightmare and tried to run faster to get away from what was chasing you? Running faster is a first order change. You realize, while you're still in the dream, it doesn't do any good to put effort into running. You've got to wake up first to end your heart-pounding race. And that's what "second order change" is all about.

Second order change wakes us up from the bad dream. Something outside of ourselves, like an alarm clock or baby crying, wakes us from our troubled sleep and forces us to act differently.

Today's verse speaks of God's Word being our "counselor." What a promise! The ultimate source of second order change is God Himself. Who else is there who can break into our bad dreams and fruitless efforts from the outside to wake us up to live victoriously?

Lord, only the wise seek Your counsel. Thank You that You never have a waiting list for our requests!

*"Assuredly, I say to you, there is no one who has
left house or parents or brothers or wife or
children, for the sake of the kingdom of God, who
shall not receive many times more in this present
time, and in the age to come eternal life."*
—LUKE 18:29–30

Aaron lost everything in choosing to follow Jesus.

Aaron grew up in an orthodox Jewish family. His
father had studied at one point to be a rabbi. Yet, at
college, Aaron met a friend who continually challenged him to search the Scriptures, Old and New, to
see if Jesus really was the "Messiah."

In reading the book of Hebrews (challenging to
many Gentiles, but extremely relevant to him), Aaron
realized for the first time that Jesus was the promised
Messiah! And it was Jesus, who now sat at the right
hand of the God of Abraham, Isaac . . . and now,
Aaron.

Aaron tried to explain his great joy to his father and
lost everything precious to him. His Dad took away his
funds for school, and he no longer could come home
without scorn.

If you've suffered righteously for claiming Christ,
this verse offers you the promise that Jesus will someday pay back, with interest, all you've ever given up
for Him!

Thank You, Lord, for sacrificing all for us.

> *I will run the course of Your commandments, for*
> *You shall enlarge my heart.*   —PS. 119:32

For many years people have run competitively. David speaks of running the course of God's commandments. This is a unique concept of running. Let's liken it to a cross-country race in which all runners begin at the same starting point, but several decide another way is better than the set course.

No matter how green the new way may be, the runner is disqualified for not sticking with the course laid out ahead of time. The runner may actually come in ahead of the rest of the contestants, but what good is it? No gold medals are given for mavericks who stray off the marked route.

In this busy world, we are all running, running, running, literally and figuratively. We need to periodically evaluate *why* we are running, *where* we are running, and *from whom* or *to whom* we are running. If we're spending too much time running away from the past or toward the future, we may well be missing the blessings on God's marked path—today.

Help me run with all speed, Lord, the course Your Son set.

"My head shall be lifted up above my enemies all around me."
                                        —PS. 27:6

It happened on the horrible battlefield Iwo Jima. During the first few days of battle, the Japanese poured murderous small arms and artillery fire from concealed sites on the highest point on this forsaken island, Mount Suribachi.

Unbearable losses and unbelievable heroism were the order of the day. And finally, incredibly, four men hoisted a large American flag on a make-shift pole on top of that killing mountain. All across the island, ignoring the danger, Marines stood up and cheered when the stars and stripes waved in the air.

The picture of these men hoisting the flag became one of the most famous pictures of World War II. Later, it would become the subject of a statue that stands in Washington, D.C. The picture of these men portrays the heroism in that noble cause. But it also shows us what David meant when he told us that God would "lift our head" above our enemies.

No matter what you're facing today, no matter how difficult the task, those difficult mountains can be taken by His power. But not without cost and not without struggle. We can only gain the courage to stay in our battles with the certainty that the same God who rescued David from his enemies and empowered our men at Iwo Jima will do the same for us.

Lord, help us remember the many sacrifices our flag represents.

> *Turn away my eyes from looking at worthless things, and revive me in Your way.*
> —PS. 119:37

Christians have a tough time walking the line between getting caught up in daily living and keeping God first.

Ella confesses, "My priority problems are in sorting out what I call the second-bests. There are so many worthy and time-consuming things, such as taking on a United Way drive. I guess I'm going to have to consider how important they're becoming compared to the time with the Lord I've been losing lately."

Sometimes listing all our activities and ranking them can help us choose God and receive His blessing of revival.

Today I will sort out my life, Lord, and prepare for Your Spirit's revival in my heart.

I will speak of Your testimonies also before kings,
and will not be ashamed.   —PS. 119:46

Dan received a call offering him an incredible opportunity.

Two years before, he had tragically lost his wife in an industrial accident that had been caused by lax safety standards. He had fought for tougher laws and sanctions as a tribute to his wife and his work was paying off.

The phone call gave him the greatest hope that change would come: It was an invitation, along with several other witnesses, to testify before a Senate committee. Can you imagine what it would be like to be called before such a body, sworn in, and then have an opportunity to tell them your story?

Dan looked forward to telling "what" had happened that had lead to his wife's death. But he also wanted to tell the Senators what had happened in his life since her death.

Dan shared not only the facts, but his testimony about how Jesus had healed him of bitterness and had been the main reason his family had stayed together and stayed strong. Dan's witness before the highest powers in this land was a wonderful picture of today's verse. Some people may have been intimidated to be so outspoken for Christ, but Dan never flinched.

May *we* never be ashamed either when our turn to speak comes, whether it's before our friends, relatives, or the highest powers.

Lord, this day I will not be ashamed of Your testimonies.

You are my portion, O Lord.
—PS. 119:57

During hard times, a mother may carefully divide the available food so each of her family members has some. More often than not, she may also secretly slip part of her portion into the others' dishes. Military personnel in war-torn countries tell incredible tales of starving children who, when given food, take only a few bites and carry the rest home, although the morsels they have eaten do little to fill their empty stomachs.

David speaks of God being our "portion." While the world may hold terrible pockets of famine and hunger, like Somolia, we are never without our spiritual portion. Our share in the feast of God's Word will one day be at a banquet hall, where we'll partake in the marriage supper of the Lamb, with Jesus in Heaven!

Thank You, God, for Your unlimited supply of love and compassion.

*Teach me good judgment and knowledge, for I
believe Your commandments.* —PS. 119:66

How many times have you heard someone say, "It
was poor judgment on my part. I guess I just didn't
have all the facts."

A high percentage of our bad judgment calls come
from not having all the facts. A referee on a basketball
court will call a judgment according to what he sees
and have the crowd rage because of what really happened. Businesses rise and fall according to judgments—and management's knowledge or lack of
knowledge.

McDonald's is known as a business with good judgment. No matter what you may think of their food, the
business has a success rate that is unequalled. This is
largely because every aspect of the business has been
carefully planned and written in a manual.

For those of us who want to live successful lives,
there is no substitute for studying and living by God's
careful plan, which is written in His manual, the Bible.

*Lord, may I, also, build every part of my life so strong in judgment
and knowledge as to endure.*

Your faithfulness endures to all generations
—PS. 119:90

The faithfulness of a mother's love, of a staunch friend, of a brother's prayers, of a father's support are all treasures we find in human relationships. Even more can we count on our Heavenly Father's love and friendship.

Almost half of this year is over. In less than two weeks, we will embark on the second half. It's a good time to stop and take stock. How are you enduring?

Many people who reach mid-life find themselves in crises. So do mid-point college students. Are you at a halfway mark, wondering if you've chosen the right path, the road to fulfillment?

As many people know, there are two symbols in Chinese for the word *crisis*. One is the symbol for *catastrophe,* the other for *opportunity.*

For the Christian, what marks the difference between catastrophe and opportunity? God's enduring, faithful love, which can keep us safe and at peace through all generations!

Even if all others prove unfaithful, Lord, I am blessed with Your steadfast commitment to me.

Your word is a lamp to my feet
—PS. 119:105

Early lamps were plant-fiber wicks and fat in a hollowed-out stone. The Romans had bronze oil lamps. Candles were an improved kind of fat lamp. In the mid-1800s, kerosene lamps came along, followed by the gas lamp and electric lights.

All these lamps had the same purpose: to cast light and dispel darkness. How exciting to think that God's Word lights up our pathway in a dark world and keeps us from stumbling!

Now that electricity has almost made other types of lamps obsolete, we might think David's metaphor isn't applicable. Not true. Once we step out of our comfortable and well-lighted homes, we still need a light for our feet. When the power fails, lamps or candles kept handy can defeat the darkness.

Thank You for Your Word, Lord, that illumines my life.

> *Your word is . . . a light to my path.*
> —PS. 119:105

My (John's) friend was drafted into the army during the Vietnam War. Fearing combat, he decided during basic training to get into the artillery. That way if he did have to go to war, he would be shooting at the enemy from behind the lines.

My friend got into the artillery. But once in Vietnam, he was assigned to be a replacement for the only artillery piece at a remote, Green Beret firebase. Instead of being miles away from the enemy, he was practically face-to-face with them.

Nighttime instilled the greatest fear in my friend. He could handle the anxiety during the day. But the inky blackness that settled over the land tripled his terror.

What a comforting verse today's selection would have been for my friend. He knew about "lighting paths." One of his jobs at night was to send up flares anytime someone thought the enemy might be coming.

God's Word acts as a light for our paths. It can help scare off unwanted thoughts in our minds and protect us from the enemy.

Lord, please shine the light of Your Word onto my path.

Uphold me according to Your word, that I may live;
and do not let me be ashamed of my hope.
　　　　　　　　　　　　　　　　—PS. 119:116

What a comfort to sing hymns that saints for centuries before us also sang. One such is, "How Firm a Foundation," recorded in John Rippon's *Selection of Hymns* (1787). Just think of it, that's the same year in which the Constitution of the new United States was drafted. James Madison and George Washington may well have sung this hymn!

While the first two stanzas introduce the thought of God laying a firm foundation, the third especially rings a message of hope down through the years.

Fear not, I am with thee; Oh, be not dismayed,
For I am thy God, and will still give thee aid;
I'll strengthen thee, help thee, and cause thee to stand,
Upheld by my righteous, omnipotent hand.

The last stanza is the heartfelt response each of us needs to make to this unspeakable blessing.

The soul that on Jesus still leans for repose
I will not, I cannot desert to his foes.
That soul, though all hell should endeavor to shake,
I'll never, no never, no never forsake!

I praise You, Lord, for Your hand that upholds me.

> *"Look upon me and be merciful to me,*
> *As Your custom is towards those who love*
> *Your name."*
>   —PS. 119:132

In the inspiring story, *Peace Child*, a godly missionary tells the story of a "custom" followed by two warring tribes he ministered to.

These neighboring tribes followed a peace-making custom during times of war. To declare a truce, a "peace child" would be given by the chief of one village to the other. As long as this child grew and lived, the peace would exist between the two feuding clans, but when the peace child died, so did the peace.

The missionary used this custom to share the wonderful message of Christ's love: By Christ's death on the cross, He became our "peace child." He was God's only Son, who put an end to sin's struggle for us. And as an eternal God, Christ lives forever to "keep that peace."

In today's verse, we see that it is God's custom to be merciful. He gives us love and peace when we may deserve just the opposite. He forgives us when we deserve punishment.

How thankful I am, Lord. You have made mercy to me Your custom.

*Direct my steps by Your word, and let no iniquity
have dominion over me.* —PS. 119:133

When something has dominion over us, it owns us.
A lot of good people are sorrowfully discovering how
easy it is for iniquity to sneak into their lives and claim
possession of them.

Some of these iniquities are obvious. But what about
the less-recognizable yet more insidious iniquities,
such as anger, regret, and fear? Anything that controls
us other than the Holy Spirit is a danger.

Eric was a three-time loser. Three times he had
tried, and failed, to kick the terrible hold that alcohol
had on his life. And yet, once more he tried, with the
help of a support group this time and the encouragement of a newfound relationship in Christ to direct His
steps, day by day.

Four years have gone by, and Eric has not had a
drink. From a three-time loser to a four-year winner,
Eric looked to Almighty God each day for the strength
to keep that drug from having dominion over him.
Though we pray that by our actions, we will never
need it, Thank you, Lord that you can give us that
same strength of heart.

Father, I ask You to direct my steps.

*Concerning Your testimonies, I have known of old
that You have founded them forever.*
—PS. 119:152

A commonly told tale is of the youngster studying history. When his teacher finished her presentation about the New World, she said, "And so Christopher Columbus founded America."

The earnest little boy said, "I didn't know America was losted."

God certainly has never been "losted." Neither have His testimonies, but the psalmist tells us that those precious testimonies of God have been founded forever.

The psalmist also implies he has known of God's enduring Word for years: "I have known *of old.*" What a reminder and challenge for us to hide God's Word in our heart and keep it there throughout each season of our life.

May I be a living monument to Your endless blessings, Lord.

Consider my affliction and deliver me.
—PS. 119:153

Franklin Delano Roosevelt, 32nd President of the United States, served in that office longer than any other president. Elected four times, he led the country for 12 years, through the worst depression and worst war the United States ever experienced.

Among his remembered sayings is this one: "Men are not prisoners of fate, but only prisoners of their own minds."

FDR, as he was known, spoke from personal knowledge. At age 39, he contracted polio. The crippling disease left him familiar with weakness. However, he did not let his affliction keep him from serving his country or enjoying life.

On March 29, 1945, FDR left for a rest at the Warm Springs Foundation in Georgia. He had written a speech for broadcast on April 13 that included, "The only limit to our realization of tomorrow will be our doubts of today. Let us move forward with strong and active faith." President Roosevelt died on the twelfth of April.

Bless me with faith to move forward and deliver me, Lord, from my afflictions.

Plead my cause and redeem me.
—PS. 119:154

Do you ever feel the whole world is against you? At times, most of us do. While living in this less-than-perfect world, we may be taken to court for a multitude of reasons. We may be ruled innocent or guilty. We may find a good lawyer or a poor one. We may face a merciful or unmerciful judge.

One of the single most outstanding benefits of being a Christian is to know we have an Advocate. When final judgment comes, with all its ramifications, Jesus Christ is going to represent us at the heavenly bar of justice. All our sins, secret and open, which would rise to condemn us to eternal punishment, have already been paid for on the cross. We can claim our redemption and eternal life through Jesus Christ.

Thank You, Lord, for the advocacy of Your Son's ministry.

I rejoice at Your word as one who finds great treasure.
                                        —PS. 119:162

What little girl or boy hasn't looked wistfully at a shimmering rainbow and wished to find the legendary pot of gold at the end of it? What adventurous child has not dreamed of pirates and treasure under the seas? How many men and women have given their lives to the pursuit of lost treasure mines in various places? On a more modern note, think of the billions of dollars people spend for lottery tickets and at casinos in hopes of striking it rich and assuring themselves a lavish future from the proceeds.

The search for treasure, whether in the form of gold doubloons or a winning ticket, often becomes an unquenchable fever. Organizations dedicated to helping gamblers control this fever offer help.

At the other end of the spectrum, David announced to the world his own personal gold strike. With rejoicing and praise, he staked a claim and reaped the benefits of the great treasure he found—God's Word.

God, thank You for the treasures in the Bible that bless me daily.

> *Lord, I hope for Your salvation, and I do Your*
> *commandment.*
> —PS. 119:166

It is highly significant that David first says he hopes for salvation, then adds that he does God's commandments. If he had reversed them, it would leave the impression that he kept the commandments because it would help him gain salvation.

Putting this scripture together with many others, we have a picture of a man who keeps the commandments, not for a reward, but because he loves his God and longs to serve Him.

Rolf was such a man. A devoted pastor and father, he spent all his life trusting Christ and working to serve Him better. I know Rolf through his children. Three are in ministry full-time and the fourth is a seminary student. *None* of them feels forced to be in ministry. They do it because they have seen a life of love and devotion modeled by their father.

Lord, give me an opportunity today to be blessed through service.

I have gone astray like a lost sheep;
Seek Your servant.

—PS. 119:176

When Lee hears the hymn, "The Ninety and Nine," she blinks back tears. Although most of her family know the Lord, one does not. He seems to delight in being the black sheep.

Lee has learned to think of him as a *lost sheep,* rather than a *black sheep.* She pictures the Good Shepherd counting the sheep and lambs in the fold. A frown puckers His smooth brow when He discovers one is missing, lost somewhere in the mountains.

When asked if the ninety and nine aren't enough, the Shepherd's voice rings, "I must go find My sheep." He sets out into the darkness, crosses raging rivers, suffers torn feet and hands, until He finds that one sheep, sick, helpless, in danger of dying.

Then, a cry that pierces heaven itself and is echoed by the angels. "Rejoice! I have found My sheep!"

Are you concerned over a lost sheep? Remember the Good Shepherd is eternally searching. Take comfort from His vigilance.

Good Shepherd, thank You for seeking and saving Your lost sheep.

July

. . . AND KEEP YOU

> *"A man's heart plans his way,*
> *But the LORD directs his steps."*
> —PROV. 16:9

Kathy had everything planned out in her life. From the time she was in junior high, she had decided that she would go to college. And she did. And after college, she'd work two years and then get married. And she did. And after two years of marriage, she and her husband would have their first child. *But they didn't.* Not after three years. Not after five years of trying every fertility expert in town.

Kathy lived by schedules, and now for the first time, she realized that she couldn't fit every decision on her daytimer. Kathy's unfulfilled plans for the time she would have a child helped her see that God was the one who ultimately was directing her steps.

It took six years and a loving Christian adoption agency to fulfill Kathy's dream of being a parent. Two years after adopting her precious son, God gave her a miracle baby girl through a much unexpected pregnancy.

There is nothing wrong with planning and organizing. Yet, we need always to keep in mind that behind all our plans lies the mighty hands of a sovereign God, a loving God, who has a purpose in directing us toward His best.

Lord, help me to plan, ultimately desiring Your will.

> *"These things I have spoken to you, that My joy*
> *may remain in you, and that your joy may be full."*
> —JOHN 15:11

I have moments of happiness," Lisa shares. "But I don't know when I've felt real joy. You know, the kind of joy a kid waiting for Christmas feels—all excitement and impatience and wonder."

"There isn't a lot of joy in my life these days," Ben says. "All I do is work, snatch a little sleep and go back to work."

Ben's and Lisa's stories aren't the exception anymore. In an age when technology should have lifted hours off our work week, most of us are working harder and longer hours than ever! However, even when we're tired and in need of rest, there is a place where we can go for refreshment, a Person to whom we can run, who can renew our hope and encouragement.

Each of us is a vessel that God wants filled with His joy. How's your level right now? Near the top? Nearly drained? Look out. Joy is not found in circumstances. It is in Jesus. Just knowing Jesus and looking to Him for help is a joy in itself.

Father, make this day more joyous than any I've known for a long time.

*"These things I have spoken to you, that you should
not be made to stumble."*   —JOHN 16:1

Notice that Jesus does not say He is warning them so
they won't stumble. Instead, He is reminding them that
others can *make* them stumble.

Have you ever thought that if you could go off by
yourself away from the world and its temptation and
troubles how single-minded you could be? Most of us
fantasize about escaping at least for a time. While most
of us won't have a tangible retreat, all believers have
an intangible "secret place" for when things get over-
whelming.

A wife who dealt with an abusive husband for years
said, "One of the worst things I experienced was being
dragged down. No matter how much I tried not to re-
taliate and yell back when my husband verbally attacked me, I could only hold out so long before I would
shout back at his level. Then I had to face my own guilt
plus his accusations that I, who was supposed to be
such a good Christian, wasn't any better than he was."

Only God can keep us from stumbling—and He will.

You know my situation, Lord. Bless me with steps that do not falter.

> *So shall I keep Your law continually, forever and ever.*
> —PS. 119:44

It was going to be a night to remember!

It was Fourth of July night. A friend had purchased several *hundred* dollars worth of fireworks (we were in a state where firecrackers are legal). And we were going to push the envelope by firing off every rocket, Roman candle, and firecracker we could.

We expected to have the best celebration ever. But our evening was cut short when one person in our group panicked and dropped their lit firecrackers right into the main box of fireworks. The resulting mini-explosion sent everyone running for cover, and created a grand finale for our fireworks before the show had barely begun!

The Fourth of July is a day to celebrate our country's birth, which is important. But it's also a good time to recall a personal "independence" day of our own. Let's take time today to celebrate the day that Jesus freed us from our sin, and set our feet on higher ground.

Lord, on this independence day, thank You for my freedom from sin.

"Ask, and it will be given to you."
—MATT. 7:7

Remember when you were a child and your best friend wanted you to stay overnight? Chances are you may have said, "You ask my mother. She'll listen to you better than if I ask."

A lot of Christians tend to feel the same way. They can't believe that their petitions to heaven will get as much attention as someone else's. Can't you almost see a group of Christians who need something from God nudging each other the way small brothers do when they say, "You ask." "No, you." Often the person viewed as most eloquent is the one frequently asked to pray for all.

It's too bad this misconception continues. God hears the stumbling tongue as clearly as the fluent one.

Perhaps you're afraid to ask God for something you desperately need, such as knowing how He wants you to serve. Maybe you're afraid He will give you what you request. Perhaps a good way to begin this prayer is to ask for freedom from uncertainty.

Lord, teach me to ask appropriately.

> *"Seek, and you will find."*
> —MATT. 7:7

Recently, PBS carried a documentary called the "Discovery of the Titanic." It was incredible to see the hundreds of man-hours and millions of dollars that went into finding a lost ship. The Titanic does hold great historic value. It became the goal of one man's life to find it, an obsession he wouldn't give up.

As I watched the underwater camera peer through the shattered remains of the ship, there was excitement around every corner. What would they find in the ship's galley? In the captain's quarters? In the great dining rooms and stately ballrooms that were once filled with life and promise?

Just imagine if we would search for God's treasures in that way. In Proverbs, we are told,

> *"Happy is the man who finds wisdom . . .*
> *for her proceeds are better than the*
> *profits of silver,*
> *And her gain than fine gold" (3:13–14).*

The treasures of the Holy Spirit are there for us to find.

———————

Thank You for the promise that when I truly seek You, I shall find You.

"Knock, and it will be opened to you."
—MATT. 7:7

For years Shawna had a troubled marriage. Finally, one day, her husband, Van, left, announcing he was never coming back.

Shawna was deeply hurt and made it clear she did not approve of Van's actions. But in spite of her feelings, Shawna decided to take a step of faith and offer him a blessing (place value on him). The more she sought counsel, knocking on the doors of the wise, the more she saw areas in her own life she could work on. Thus, she began feeling less anger toward her husband.

Shawna and Van have been back together for two years now. She and Van credit the turnaround in their marriage to her positive actions.

God often asks us to choose to act despite our feelings. We may not *feel* like knocking, or asking for God's help. Or we may not believe God will change us or our loved ones or our circumstances. As we knock, every door will not open; some will stay closed. But it is vital to remember that we will never be inside a door if we do not lift up our hands to knock.

Lord, it takes faith to believe that when I knock, You will answer.

A man will be as a hiding place from the wind.
—ISA. 32:2

Wind is one of the most powerful forces of God's creation. It can be gentle or tempestuous. It can cool or destroy. It can fan fires or sweeten the air.

When the wind begins to reach gale force, people often search for hiding places, for themselves and for their property. Those unfortunate enough to get caught in a desert sandstorm seek shelter behind gnarled trees or in caves.

Mighty winds of change have swept the world in the last few decades. Beliefs and practices unacceptable and hidden have demanded not only recognition, but acceptance. Things Christians formerly ignored or didn't discuss are thrust into homes via the media. Has there ever been a time when we needed a hiding place more than now? The winds of permissiveness and sin continue to blow.

The good news is that the "wind" of the Holy Spirit is also sweeping the world. He offers the hiding place we so desperately need.

Thank You for the blessing of refuge in You, God.

A man will be as . . . a cover from the tempest.
—ISA. 32:2

Another major hurricane smashed into the Florida coast. The news media captured pictures of thousands of people fleeing the coastline, and hundreds more, afterward, who wished they had.

The universal feeling of the people who stayed and endured was fear. During the most destructive time of the storm, when it seemed like a railroad car was crashing through their homes, they felt helpless and with no place of shelter.

When the Disciples feared for their lives amidst a storm, they ran to a sleeping Jesus. His answer to their fears was to calm the waters: "Peace, be still!" He then told them that He was their shelter for the storm. (See Mark 4:35–41.)

It's not the size of the storm that matters but the strength of our shelter. Isaiah 32:2 offers a wonderful promise that we can find a cover from the tempests of life. Whether it's a storm of controversy or slander whipped up by Satan or simply an unwelcomed wind of change, we can weather the storm inwardly because of the strength Jesus gave us.

Thank You, Lord, that You are our shelter from any storm.

> *A man will be . . . as rivers of water in a dry place.*
> —ISA. 32:2

Out in Arizona, it happened more than once. A single wagon in a wagon train would pull out of line to escape the hot, dusty trail. And in spite of the warnings of others, would head "toward the horizon and *water!*"

Those same people would eventually find out that the "water" that danced on the horizon was nothing but a mirage. Instead of dipping their tin cups into thirst-quenching refreshment, they would die choking on sand.

It's a terrible picture: people lured to their death by a mirage. But it happens every day. Sexual immorality that results in AIDS, uncontrolled workaholism that leads to a heart attack, unbridled drinking that results in carnage on the freeway. Many people are drawn by something that looks good from a distance, only to find out that it's end is death.

Thank God we can find, and can become to others, a life-giving spring. Those who know and trust Jesus have this "well of living water" springing up inside their life. They can stay on the road to health and fulfillment and avoid the deadly detours others take.

Lord, keep my life filled to overflowing with Your love. Then I will find Your protection, and be a source of provision to others.

A man will be . . . as the shadow of a great rock in a weary land.
                                                    —ISA. 32:2

Nearly fifteen years ago, when Cindy and I (John) dated, she was living in Phoenix, Arizona, and I was living in Tucson, two hours away. For someone in a hurry to see his true love, the drive between the two cities seemed an eternity. The road was flat and monotonous, with only a few turns and no scenery to brag of, with one exception.

About halfway to Cindy's house, I could see a bump arising from the flat landscape. A spot would begin to grow and build on the horizon, until a great rock formation jutted out of the sand: Shiprock.

For miles I could see that peak inch upward as I inched toward it. Then, for miles, it stayed in my rearview mirror, slipping out of sight at a glacier pace. Every trip, Shiprock was a reminder that I was halfway to seeing Cindy. It helped to make the time pass more quickly.

I'm sure that Shiprock was the kind of place written about in today's verse—a great rock that provides shadows of relief from the heat and sun for a weary traveler. Jesus, too, is a rock like Shiprock and the rock of Isaiah. The Rock of our Salvation, He offers us the blessings of refreshment, encouragement, and peace.

I praise You, Lord, for Your comforting shadow.

> *"I cried out to God with my voice—*
> *To God with my voice;*
> *And He gave ear to me."*
> —PS. 77:1

Years ago, I (John) ran the scoreboard for the football games at Texas Christian University. While the job didn't pay very much, it did provide an incredible seat in the press box and a free lunch—both hard for a hungry college student to pass up.

I'll never forget the first time I saw Texas A & M come to the TCU stadium. With their rich heritage of winning football, they have tremendous support all over Texas, which was evidenced when the ball was kicked off. The stands below looked like a sea of red, not purple and white!

That day, I got a small taste of what God must hear when the praises and petitions of his people sail upward. For nearly four hours, seated in one of the tallest (not biggest) pressboxes in any collegiate stadium, I heard a roaring of thunder continually shooting up. The voices of the A & M fans were so loud, they shot up where we were and drowned out nearly everything else!

God doesn't need for us to shout. We can whisper and He still hears our prayers. But the next day in church, I realized, as never before, how our voices do carry upward to the God of all heaven.

Thank You, Lord that You hear us when we cry out.

The ears of those who hear will listen.
—ISA. 32:3

Deafened by an explosion in the mine where he worked, Angelo faced a suddenly silent world. No more early morning birdsongs. No clatter of machinery or children's laughter. None of the sounds he had taken for granted all his life now penetrated the soundproof curtain that surrounded him.

Angelo soon found he had a second foe, one much worse than the loss of his hearing. Bitterness threatened to corrode his very soul. *How could a loving God let such a thing happen to him?* he wondered.

After the first shock, his wife clasped her arms around him and simply held him. Then she wrote him a message: "We can thank God it wasn't your eyes, or your strong arms, or your powerful legs. Yes, God has been good."

Lord, is there someone I can encourage with the blessing of Your peace?

> *"Why do you say . . .*
> *'My way is hidden from the LORD,*
> *And my just claim is passed over by my God.'"*
> —ISA. 40:27

Have you ever doubted God? If you're honest, then like most of us (me included), you'd have to say yes. And did you know that when we doubt God, it almost always is because of two primary factors?

First, Isaiah tells us that those who doubted in his day complained, "My way is hidden from the Lord." This word *hidden* is used in the Old Testament to represent a cloud passing in front of the sun. In other words, the people felt God somehow couldn't see through some barrier to where His people were suffering.

The people's second complaint was, "The justice due me escapes the notice of my God." If they first doubted God's ability to help, here they go even further. Perhaps God *can* help them, they think, *but perhaps He simply doesn't want to.* He could intervene, but He doesn't choose to and our rights are being violated.

Have you ever doubted God's ability or desire to help you in the midst of a trial? We'll see tomorrow what Isaiah's answer was to such doubts.

Thank You, Lord, for the security we have to express our doubts.

*"Have you not known?
Have you not heard?"*
—ISA. 40:28

In answer to the doubts the people were bringing about God, Isaiah responds with a rhetorical question. If it's been a while since you've studied English grammar, perhaps you'll remember that this is the type of question that assumes a positive answer. In other words, it's a question that answers it's own question, with a positive. "Do you not know?" *Of course we do!* "Have you not heard?" *Of course we have!*

Isaiah offers reminders of truth long since taught, not fresh insights designed to combat doubt, saying they already *knew* the answer to their doubts. As the rest of the passage points out, they have an everlasting, mighty, gracious, compassionate God who actively wants to help them

So much for our doubts. Our God can and will act on behalf of His loved ones in His time.

Thank You, Lord, that we never have to doubt You.

> *Blessed is the man who walks not in the counsel of*
> *the ungodly.*
> —PS. 1:1

Albert Schweitzer, who has been called one of the greatest Christians of his time, wrote of his gratitude that in his youth "so many people gave me something or were something to me without knowing it."

We sense the humility of a man who in turn gave the world everything within him. It would be interesting to have a list of those Dr. Schweitzer remembered with such fondness and appreciation.

Every day, Christians struggle with the counsel of the ungodly through the media and from peers. A little exercise to counteract this pressure is to close your eyes and remember as far back as you can, to those who, as Dr. Schweitzer described, gave or were something to you without ever knowing it.

Perhaps an elementary school teacher praised some beginning ability. Maybe a coach encouraged you. Perhaps it was the quiet grandmother at church who loved you and prayed for you. Each may have contributed to helping shape your life as it now is.

God, Your counsel is always what we need, but I thank You for the wise counsel of friends and family, as well.

*Blessed is the man who . . . [does not stand] in the
path of sinners.*
—PS. 1:1

It would be wonderful and make life easier if every time we came to a crossroads in life a great big sign confronted us: "This Is the Path of Danger." We could then flee, or at least know that if we walked that path it would be by deliberate choice.

There is no sign designating the path of sinners. However, warning signs do exist and, if we live close to our Lord, we can recognize them.

The psalm doesn't say we shouldn't walk in the path. It goes beyond that to state we are not even to *stand* in that path, let alone take steps along it.

The best way to avoid being caught on the wrong path is to practice prayer. Back in the 1600s, Thomas Fuller advised, "Prayer should be the key of the day and the lock of the night."

What imagery! A key opens up every new day with all its possibilities. A lock secures us against the night and its pitfalls. It leaves us cozy and warm on the inside, safe from battering storms and temptations.

May I never tarry in the path of sinners, Father.

> *Blessed is the man who . . . [does not sit] in the seat*
> *of the scornful.*
> —PS. 1:1

Recently, something happened that was new to the annals of sports. It didn't involve a catch. Nor did it involve any points scored. It was a foul, but it never occurred on the play field. Give up?

In one National Basketball city, there was a man (a lawyer it turned out), who was so belligerent, vulgar, loud, and scornful game after game, he actually had his season tickets revoked. Of course, he filed a lawsuit in protest!

Today's verse tells us that we are not to "sit in the seat of the scornful." This man epitomized someone who used his words to try and tear down . . . not build up. And in a miraculous vindication of common sense (rare in our court system nowadays), he did lose his seats, and had to pay the team's legal fees for the team attorneys!

David goes beyond simply saying that it's wrong to blast others with our words. He focuses on the positive. The person who refuses to use this killer weapon will be blessed of God for not being scornful. That's a blessing we can lay hold of, if we'll just lay off our negative words!

Thank You, Lord, for putting healthy boundaries around proper speech.

"Ask for the old paths, where the good way is, and walk in it; then you will find rest for your souls."
—JER. 6:16

Have you ever been so bone-weary from physical work you wondered if you could even stand up again? Do you recall being so mentally stressed that if one more thing went wrong, you felt you'd run away from home? Are you more soul-sick with the way the world has turned?

Jeremiah, a mighty prophet of God, certainly experienced every frustration and obstacle any Christian witness could encounter. In desperation he must have cried to his Master, many times, for help. Imagine Jeremiah's renewed energy and rest for his soul when he received God's answers. Jeremiah's work was to point people back to the old paths, the good way.

Do you need to find your way back that you might find rest for your soul?

When my soul is sick, Lord, give me the rest that will heal it.

July 20 – REFUGE FOR THE OPPRESSED

The Lord also will be a refuge for the oppressed . . . in times of trouble.
—PS. 9:9

The Old Testament is filled with stories of oppression—brother ruling brother, captivity, and slavery. Satan uses his power to oppress and laughs at the misery he creates.

Citizens of some countries flee from oppression, others have overthrown their government.

Sometimes we see oppression as happening to someone else, people far away. However, *any time a group or individual takes control of another person or group of people, in a way that creates a master/slave situation, we have oppression in our midst.*

Family members are guilty at times. So are friends. Not to the point of depriving one of the basic necessities, but by stripping people of their value. To these people, the Lord offers refuge, a haven, sanctuary. If you are experiencing any type of oppression, turn to your Lord for refuge.

What joy, Lord, to know You shelter the oppressed.

For the needy shall not always be forgotten; the expectation of the poor shall not perish forever.
—PS. 9:18

A letter appeared on the bulletin board of a small church. Written by a child in crooked letters on a sheet of cheap paper it said,

"Thank you for Christmas. Mama said we wouldn't have one this year. You must care a lot about people to bring all the food and toys and clothes. It is the only and best Christmas my brothers and sisters and I can remember. God bless you."

This family had expected nothing and so the unexpected caring of total strangers apparently fell on them with the surprise, joy, and wonder that marked the first Christmas.

David separated the needy from the poor. He must have observed a lot of need as well as those who were merely poor. Palaces and penthouses often house needy people. We all have needs. What kind of blessing do you need today?

We know we have not been forgotten, Lord, and praise You for it.

You observe trouble and grief.
—PS. 10:14

At times, it may be easy to think that God is some-how remote and far away from our troubles, but that's never the case. David's words remind us that God does see our trouble and grief. God is much more than a passive observer. Jesus wept over an entire city, and even cried at the death of a friend.

On this day, remind yourself several times that He sees you; He cares for you; He's protecting you. We are never out of His sight. Praise the Lord!

Thank You, Lord, for being more than a mere observer of our lives.

The helpless commits himself to You.
—PS. 10:14

Catherine Marshall, in her book *Beyond Ourselves,* revealed that her most spectacular answers to prayer followed her recognition of helplessness.

Mrs. Marshall had been bed-ridden for months, despite constant prayer and medical attention. She finally received a pamphlet about a missionary, who at the end of eight years of invalidism, was worn out with praying for health to serve God. In desperation, she at last told God that she was giving up. If He wanted her to be an invalid for the rest of her life, she'd accept it and cling to Him.

Within two weeks, the woman was well.

When Catherine Marshall dared to pray that prayer of relinquishment, recovery began. Others who have come to the place where God was not just *the* answer but the *only* answer have reported similar experiences and results.

Why is this so? Aware of his smallness and God's greatness, the helpless gives his whole heart, not just part of it.

_____

Today, Lord, I recognize my own helplessness. I need You to take care of each situation I encounter.

You are the helper of the fatherless.
—PS. 10:14

Todd and Kenneth both lost their dads when they were small. Todd's dad died in a car accident; Kenneth, Sr. in a plane crash. Both mothers did their best to raise the boys. However, there was one big difference in their approaches that affected the way Todd and Kenneth grew up.

"I missed not having a dad so much," Todd says. "At first, I'd ask when Daddy was coming back, but after Mom explained he was in heaven I stopped asking. At first I didn't notice how the pictures of Dad gradually disappeared or how seldom Mom mentioned him. Sometimes I had trouble remembering what he looked like. Then, I felt guilty."

"I missed Dad, too," Kenneth shares. "Yet in a way, it was almost like he still lived at our house, we just couldn't see him. Mom talked about him a lot. When I did something well, she always told me how proud he'd be."

God the Father helps the fatherless and blesses them.

———————

Lord, teach me to know You as Father.

"When you pray, do not use vain repetitions as the heathen do. Your Father knows the things you have need of before you ask Him." —MATT. 6:7–8

Christians sometimes have trouble separating the idea of praying the same prayer over and over, which may appear to be vain repetition, and pouring out their hearts in continual prayer.

Have you ever heard people from other cultures who chant? If you listen carefully, you'll discover their words may be the same few, repeated again and again or only slightly varied.

In Matthew, chapter six, Jesus gave us a model prayer. It covers everything for which we need to pray:

- praise of our Father
- recognition of God's will in our life
- petitions for our needs, for forgiveness, and deliverance
- recognition of God's eternal might.

Bless me with the ability to adapt this prayer to my needs, O Lord.

> *"Come to Me, all you who labor and are heavy laden, and I will give you rest."* —MATT. 11:28

There is evidence that people who never experience hard work seldom appreciate rest. On the other hand, sometimes we overwork, so much so that we cannot rest even when the tasks are finished.

Good transitions from the intensity of hard work and bedtime are essential. Too many tired business people have discovered the folly of working right up until time for sleep, only to toss and turn while the subconscious stubbornly hangs onto some unsolved, knotty problem.

Jesus lived in a world of hard, physical work. He companioned with fishermen and others who made their living by the sweat of their brow. They recognized labor for what it was and were laden with heavy burdens imposed by an unfriendly Roman government. Jesus' promise of rest must have been heralded with cheers. It still is.

Thank You, Lord, for the rest that only comes from You.

[Cast] all your care upon Him, for He cares for You.
—1 PETER 5:7

Donna carried the weight of the universe on her shoulders. At times, concern and worry over family and friends made her feel kin to the mythological Atlas, doomed to forever hold up the sky. Everyone brought their troubles to Donna—and left them on her doorstep.

Time after time Donna turned her cares over to the Master she loved, trusted and served. How marvelous to have a God who cares so much for us that He invites us to bring all our cares to Him and leave them with Him.

It isn't a cop-out to do this. God is God. He is far better prepared to deal with our cares than we are. His eternal vision sees around corners we don't even know are ahead.

The blessing of Your accepting my concerns is great, Lord. Thank You.

He will guard the feet of His saints.
—1 SAM. 2:9

Peter Marshall, a young Scottish immigrant, pastored the New York Avenue Presbyterian Church in Washington, D.C. and served as Chaplain to the U.S. Senate.

The promise in 1 Samuel was real in Peter Marshall's early life. Catherine Marshall (Peter's wife) recorded in his biography, *A Man Called Peter*, a dark night Peter decided to take a short cut across the Scottish moors. He knew an unused limestone quarry lay near, but believed he could miss it.

Out of the blackness came an urgent call. "Peter!"

He stopped and asked who was there and went on. A second call stopped him again. Peter stumbled, reached out—and found nothing. God had guarded his feet. One more step ahead lay nothing but space and death.

Peter Marshall interpreted this experience to mean God had work for him. In later years similar escapes from danger confirmed his belief.

We may never know how many times God has stopped a rushing car from killing us. Or stopped us from walking a dark and dangerous path. It is impossible to count the guardian-type blessings we receive.

Thank You for protecting me, Lord, and guarding my footsteps.

If we confess our sins, He is faithful and just to forgive us our sins and to cleanse us from all unrighteousness.
—1 JOHN 1:9

A man looked back on his life and bowed his head in both pain and amazement. "When I think of the hundreds of times I sinned against God and those who loved me, I can't believe how they all forgave me. My mother never gave up on me."

When he looked up, a smile had replaced the marks of agony. "Thank God, for His faithfulness, and for the faithfulness of my family, especially Mother."

It is hard at times to believe that God waits patiently until we see how sinful we are, then confess and receive His cleansing. Even the most wonderful followers aren't exempt from impatience, fear, and discouragement. All the time we're struggling, God is right there encouraging.

Thank You, Father, for Your faithfulness to forgive and encourage me.

*Keep me as the apple of Your eye; hide me under
the shadow of Your wings.*   —PS. 17:8

If you visit Washington state, you'll learn that there
are all kinds of apples—Delicious, Jonathan, Granny
Smith, Transparent—each with its own peculiarities.

When David asked God to keep him as the apple of
His eye, we can imagine he had in mind a perfect and
polished specimen of apple, a joy to behold as well as
to taste. This is a great description. David knew that
God had invested a lot more in him than a gardener
puts into an orchard—which is a considerable investment given that planting, fertilizing, eliminating disease and insects must all occur before the harvest.

David further boldly asked to be hidden under the
shadow of God's wings. He recognized how important
it was to be close to his Heavenly Father.

As the beloved of God, under the shadow of His
wings--and as the apples of God's eye, the seeds of
great faith lie within us.

*Thank You, Lord, for keeping me as the apple of Your eye, and hid-
den under the shadow of Your wing.*

You will keep him in perfect peace, whose mind is stayed on You, because he trusts in You.
—ISA. 26:3

In this world of little or no peace, does Isaiah's promise really apply to us now, all these years after he gave it?

Absolutely. God *will* keep us in perfect peace if we meet two conditions.

First, the perfect peace promise is only for a specific group of persons: those whose minds are "stayed" on God. We don't often see this word used in such a way, but it clearly indicates the need to keep our minds focused on God in all things, through all things, for all things.

The second qualification is actually an explanation of the first. Some people's minds are fixed on God but only to prove that He doesn't exist. It grows obvious that our minds must be fixed on God because of our trust in Him.

If you find yourself torn and afraid, wishing you lived in a different time, turn your mind to God, the giver of perfect peace.

Perfect peace can be ours and will be when our minds are focused on God in trust and expectancy.

August

THE LORD MAKE
HIS FACE TO SHINE
UPON YOU

Make Your face shine upon Your servant.
—PS. 119:135

If you have ever taught a class of children, you will remember how they turned shining clean faces toward you at the beginning of the day or class.

Part of what makes children's faces shine and eyes sparkle is anticipation. Perhaps a promised treat or a new story or an upcoming picnic. It really is true that at least half of the fun of a special happening is thinking about it and planning for it.

During the month of August, which for most of us is the sunniest of the year, we'll explore some of the ways the Lord makes His face shine on us. Note that the verse doesn't say that He lets or allows it to shine. *He makes it shine by choice.*

For the blessed sunshine You put into my heart, Lord, I give You thanks.

> *"You did not choose Me, but I chose you and*
> *appointed you that you should go and bear fruit,*
> *and that . . . whatever You ask the Father in My*
> *name He may give you."*   —JOHN 15:16

There is no record in the world that tells how many lives have been changed by this verse. However, Blake's story is representative.

Abandoned at birth, raised in an institution, farmed out to foster homes again and again, Blake knew he had to be worthless. Time after time, just when he thought he'd be adopted, things fell apart and he ended up back at the institution.

When Blake met Jesus Christ and heard about God's love, he found it incredibly hard to believe. If no human could find anything in him to love, how could Almighty God? It wasn't until Blake read this verse that he could accept God's love and his own value to the Creator.

"*I* chose parents many times," Blake shares. "When they refused to choose me, I slumped back into despair. The idea that Jesus actually picked me out for His own has changed my life. You can count on me serving Him from now on."

Thank You for choosing me, Lord. You make me see my own worth to You and others.

He said to them, "Follow Me, and I will make you fishers of men."
                                                        —MATT. 4:19

Andrew and Simon Peter cast their net into the sea. Fishermen by trade, the smell of salt water and fish permeated their clothes. Wrinkles at the corners of far-seeing eyes cut into their tanned faces.

When Jesus walked toward them one day, the Bible recorded no chitchat or preliminary, "How's fishing?" He merely looked at the two working men and said, "Follow Me, and I will make you fishers of men."

Did He smile with the invitation? Did a shine in His steady eyes make it more a commandment than an invitation? In any case, Jesus' invitation must have been compelling, because they dropped everything and followed Him.

A little later, Jesus invited James and John in the same way. They, too, walked away from their work without a backward glance.

When the Lord makes His face shine upon us, unusual things happen. We may also "leave our nets" to become fishers of men.

May I immediately respond to my glimpses of Your shining face, Lord.

> *The Lord lives! Blessed be my Rock! Let the God of*
> *my salvation be exalted.*　　　　—PS. 18:46

One of the strongest appeals to the minds of thinking people of other religions is that Christianity is built on the concept of a living, ever-present God, rather than a long-dead prophet or a flock of gods. It must be difficult to worship some deity who isn't around anymore.

Most Christians secretly wish they could have the availability to Jesus that His disciples did. To actually see His smile, feel His hand in blessing, be able to talk to Him face-to-face.

Long before the birth of Jesus, David held fast to a living Lord, a Rock, a God that brought salvation and was to be exalted. Many times David felt his Master's smile and knew God's face shone upon him. Now, in a rare moment of ecstasy, David cries out words that echo and re-echo through all the long years between his day and ours.

I know You live, Lord, and I lift my heart in praise to You.

The fruit of the Spirit is love.
—GAL. 5:22

Here is another passage that should be studied regularly, not just read. For the next few days, we'll look at the fruits of the Spirit Paul promised to faithful saints.

Earlier we talked about all the things a fruit grower must do to encourage perfect, delicious fruit. Have you ever considered how important it is for us to follow the same procedure so we can harvest these fruits of the Spirit?

Clear the ground. Rocks of resentment, smoldering stumps of anger, and the like, have to be dug out and hauled away.

Prepare the soil. Few fields have perfect soil. The preparation of repentance will build rich dirt.

Plant. The Holy Spirit grows best when the weeds of doubt and discouragement are pulled.

Tend. Consistent prayer and worship maintain the growth.

Allow time to grow then reap your harvest of love.

Master Gardener, stir the hard-caked earth of my heart so Your Spirit will thrive in me.

> *The fruit of the Spirit is . . . joy.*
> —GAL. 5:22

We've already talked a lot about joy this year. It's an oft-discussed subject in classes, a prime topic for sermons, and an all-round wonderful word. It makes pleasant feelings dance in our hearts and anticipation lighten our minds.

Over 200 years ago, Charles Wesley wrote "Love Divine, All Loves Excelling." In the very first stanza he included these words, "Joy of heaven to earth come down."

The best part about joy is that we don't have to wait for the return of Jesus in order to experience it. When we choose to march at His side, He will never leave us, we are cleansed, His Spirit continually guides us and we learn to lift our voices in wonder, love and praise.

The joy You offer, Lord, eclipses all other joy.

The fruit of the Spirit is . . . peace.
—GAL. 5:22

It seems hard to believe the numerous times peace has been won through strength. In the early 1980s, President Reagan kept a strong military presence and stance towards Communism. This past Summer, when I (Gary) was in Russia, a top Kremlin official told me what the Russians thought of Reagan's consistent policy of "Walk softly, but carry a big stick!"

"We respected Reagan," the leader said. "We didn't agree with him often, but his tough stance made us turn our faces towards peace."

Although there are many reasons for the fall of Communism, and many opinions on what President Reagan's role was in its demise, one thing is unquestionable. Because of Reagan's and, later, President Bush's commitment to strength, we live in a safer world today than at any time since the cold war began.

A similar principle exists in our spiritual lives. For as we strengthen our character and develop the self-control that bears the "fruits of the Spirit," we will be reaping inner peace and rest! What a blessing that the God who leveled Sodom and Jericho never uses His strength except to build a lasting peace!

Thank You, Lord, for Your strength and peace.

> *The fruit of the Spirit is . . . longsuffering.*
> —GAL. 5:22

It's hard to see how longsuffering can be a fruit of the Spirit. Or how if God is making His face shine upon us, longsuffering has any business getting into the act.

Webster defines longsuffering as "long and patient endurance" of troubles or offense. With this insight, one application can be honoring parents who may not deserve honor or blessing.

"Bless my parents? Are you kidding? After what they did to me? After what they put me through?" you may be saying after you read this. This is where the longsuffering comes in.

Let's be clear. Making a decision to honor parents doesn't mean allowing our alcoholic father to drive our children across town. Nor does it require a daily call to our verbally abusive mother when each call is an invitation to attack. It means we decide to attach value to them and not to dishonor them because of their alcoholism or temper.*

Lord, bless me with the gift of longsuffering that I might stay close to You.

*The Blessing, Chapter 13

The fruit of the Spirit is . . . kindness.
—GAL. 5:22

Many years ago, Mary Dow Brine wrote a poem titled "Somebody's Mother" that became a common sermon illustration for Mother's Day. The poem tells of a ragged old woman slowly going home on a chill winter day. She stands in the snow at the crossing, afraid to step forward and overlooked by the passers-by.

A group of boys pass her. Then one boy stops and helps the old woman across the busy street.

When he gets back to his friends he tells them that even though she's old and slow and poor, the little woman is "somebody's mother." He adds that he hopes someone will help *his* mother if ever she is far away and poor and old.

That night, somebody's mother prays that God will be kind to somebody's son who showed such great kindness to her in her time of need.

Seldom does a congregation hear this story-poem and remain dry-eyed. Each member can visualize the boy who helped the stranger. Most added a prayer for their own mothers that resembled the boy's wish. What kindness can you do today?

Lord, help me pass on this fruit of the Spirit today.

> *The fruit of the Spirit is . . . goodness.*
> —GAL. 5:22

Take a few moments to think of a few people who truly carry goodness as a fruit of the Spirit.

Now consider why they came to mind. What is it that makes these lives seem outstanding? Is it humility, a Christlike attitude, a giving lifestyle that marks them as special?

A high percentage of the truly good Christians who live out their lives in service and die knowing their heavenly reward is assured are never recognized in this world for their contribution. Goodness doesn't demand medals and public ceremonies to perpetuate itself.

We cannot be good simply by choice, no matter how hard we try. Only by accepting the Holy Spirit's direction will we qualify for or receive this special blessing. It is worth seeking.

Fill me with goodness, Lord, not for my glory, but to lead others to You.

The fruit of the Spirit is . . . faithfulness.
—GAL. 5:22

Years ago a man visited Yellowstone Park and marveled at the display Old Faithful put on regularly. The geyser with its splashing, foaming waters made such an impression on him, he vowed to return with his family.

Years passed before he fulfilled the vow. In the meantime, various adverse conditions had affected Yellowstone Park. Earthquakes and fire left their mark. The man and his family clung to his memory of Old Faithful.

They arrived and waited. The geyser shot into the air but not with the regularity the man had remembered. Disgruntled that it had let him down, the man muttered, "Let's go. Old Faithful isn't."

Let's face it. There aren't many things, or people, so faithful we can be sure they will never let us down. However, faithfulness as a fruit of the Spirit is greatly to be desired.

Are you practicing this fruit of the Spirit?

I long to be faithful, God; may Your Spirit bless me.

The fruit of the Spirit is . . . gentleness.
—GAL. 5:22, 23

Gentleness is often seen as weakness. Sometimes gentle people are regarded as harmless or ineffective. However, truly gentle people are those who have determined that the benefits of gentle behavior are worth the effort required to develop a gentle disposition.

Think of the proverbs advising gentle answers in times of anger and confusion. Anyone with the strength to speak gently when being attacked is definitely not a weakling.

It is always exciting to hear the testimony of an athlete or public figure who attributes his success to his mother. It is even more interesting to meet that mother. Many of us have been startled to discover a quiet lady rather than a driving force. Those who employ gentleness wield powerful influence.

Life doesn't always deal gently with us. It shakes us up and sets us down hard again and again. Often we pray that friends or family will treat us more gently. God sent His Son Jesus as an example of gentleness. Even when people fail us, His gentleness soothes us.

Lord, create in me a gentle spirit that reflects Your Son.

The fruit of the Spirit is . . . self-control.
—GAL. 5:22, 23

I can't control my kids," a harried father confessed. "They don't even try to exercise self-control. Our home is in chaos."

The man's friend bit his lip. How could he say, even in the kindest way, "Hey, those kids are a direct reflection of you. Until you can control your own temper and tongue, chaos will continue in your home."

There are times when the highest self-control is needed. If you are not already practicing this attribute, you may find it tough to bear peace and comfort rather than worry yourself to a sickroom, to refrain from yelling at your boss, or stay cool in a crisis.

Do you need the gift of self-control? Pray for it.

Father, I commit myself to You. Please teach me self-control.

> *[Jesus Christ,] whom having not seen you love.*
> —1 PETER 1:8

Long before Jan met her Uncle Richard, she felt she knew him. He had been away on foreign service assignments since Jan was little. However, the photograph of him and stories told by the family helped Jan learn to love her uncle, sight unseen. When he finally visited, any awkward or uncomfortable gap that could have existed had already been bridged.

One of the excuses non-Christians use when approached with the message of Jesus is, "But how can I know Him when I've never seen Him?"

The answer lies in the same pattern Jan's mother used to teach her daughter to love an unknown relative. She talked about him. She told of shared experiences. She introduced Jan to the worthy qualities in Richard's life and, a little at a time, knowledge of the kind of person Richard was became solid knowledge in Jan's heart and mind. In addition, Jan's mother stressed how much Richard had always loved Jan. We learn to love God in the same way.

You may be unseen, God, but You are not unknown to Your children.

*I have no greater joy than to hear that my children
walk in truth.*
                                    —3 JOHN 4

For nearly twenty years, I have worn something that is a constant reminder of my (John's) past. It's a simple silver ring, shaped in the symbol of the early church's greeting. Some call it a fish sign.

This ring does two things for me.

First, it's a visual aid for what I want to teach my children. I tell them that my wedding ring proclaims that I belong to "Mommy" for life, and my "fish" ring says that I belong to Jesus for life. And it also holds another meaning for me.

Like the apostle John, this John also has no greater joy than picking up a ringing phone and hearing the voice of a friend I worked with years ago. This particular friend, a former Young Life campaigner, is still walking with the Lord. In 1973, my friend and almost forty students took me out to dinner on my birthday and gave me the ring I wear. Some of them still make my day by calling, all these years later.

Is there someone that you could encourage and thank for their investment in your life? Your call could be just the dose of encouragement that person needs today.

_____

Lord, thank You for the encouragement You give us from memories past.

"Behold, I send My messenger before Your face,
who will prepare Your way before You.
—MARK 1:2

The blessing of being a messenger for God is one of the richest and most rewarding blessings we can receive. Yet often we either do not recognize the opportunities for, or are unwilling to accept the responsibility of, being God's messengers.

Pony Express riders were diligent messengers who knew theirs was a hazardous assignment, but also knew the mail must get through.

The U.S. Postal Service doesn't face the hazards of the early Pony Express riders, but its goal is also to get the message from the sender to the receiver, regardless of weather or indistinct handwriting.

As Christians, we face mountains, valleys, hostility, and stormy weather. Sometimes we're most needed in the middle of the night, on our holidays, or during time we've reserved to be alone. Yet carrying God's message cannot be delayed.

Bless me, Father, with new understanding of what being Your messenger means.

*You will also declare a thing, and it will be
established for you; so light will shine on
your ways.*

—JOB 22:28

Job's friend Eliphaz the Temanite may not have been the world's greatest comforter, but he did have some pretty smart things to say. This is one of them. When we follow God, His light *will* shine, not just in us, but on our ways.

The closer we get, the brighter our enlightenment, until we step into His presence and the chandelier-like glow.

Light comes in two different ways. It can be generated from within, the way an electric bulb generates it. It can also be reflected, as by a mirror. Christians need it both ways. We must be power houses, in which the Holy Spirit creates light as well as reflectors of Jesus and His standards.

What better blessing can we have, Lord, than the light of Your presence?

> *His lamp shone upon my head, . . . by His light I*
> *walked through darkness.*   —JOB 29:3

Job is so much like the rest of us that it's easy to relate to him. Part of the time, despite his affliction, he praises God. He also has his down times. This is one of them. Job longed for the months past when God watched over him and shone a spotlight to drive away the darkness in his life.

Ginger was someone, like Job, who saw plenty of darkness: a failed marriage, a difficult childhood. She was even talked into pulling out all of her teacher's salary and investing in a limited oil partnership, which lost every cent of her money.

But like Job, she never walked so far into the dark that the light of her knowledge of God's Word didn't light her path. At times, it was a weak light. But it kept her heart steady until better times.

What an encouragement for each of us to prepare for difficult times by hiding the light of God's Word in our hearts! Like a "charged up" flashlight, it's ready to keep us from stumbling!

Dear Lord, please bless me with the light of Your Word.

*He causes the grass to grow for the cattle, and
vegetation for the service of man, that he may
bring forth food from the earth, and wine, . . .
oil, . . . and bread.*   —PS. 104:14, 15

When God smiles on the world and makes His face
shine, crops grow and mankind is fed. David speaks of
bringing forth food and mentions oil to make his face
shine.

This point may not seem significant now but it did
at that time. Men wore beards and carefully oiled
them, plus their hair and faces. Women oiled their
bodies.

Oil was and continues to be respected for use in
many ways. Oil is for anointing and setting apart chosen ones who will serve God in special ways. It is also
used to anoint the heads of those who are sick.

In the New Testament, Christ used elements of creation to make various points while He was teaching,
like a grain of mustard seed, a fig tree, rocky soil. We
can thank God for His creation that brings Him glory
in so many ways and holds special value for us.

*Lord, make my face shine from Your liberal application of the oil
of joy.*

> *But the path of the just is like the shining sun, that*
> *shines ever brighter unto the perfect day.*
> —PROV. 4:18

It has been said that a great blessing is our inability to see more than a step or two ahead, for what lies in the future may be so grim we would lose heart and turn back.

In this verse, Solomon boldly promises that not only will the path of the just be brightly lighted, it will shine like the sun and grow brighter and brighter until the final meeting between God and His children.

When young Joel accepted the Lord into his heart, the grass looked greener, the sky bluer, and life brighter. Yet when he reached old age, his testimony was that through the years that brightness became ever brighter.

Perhaps this is a time when your path is murky and unclear. You've tried your best and still things aren't the way you want them to be. If so, now is the exact moment to turn to your Heavenly Father and ask for His sun and Son to shine on you.

Heavenly sunshine is never rationed, even on gloomy days.

*The people who walked in darkness have seen a
great light; those who dwelt in the land of the
shadow of death, upon them a light has shined.*
—ISA. 9:2

It is easy to read this well-known scripture and relate
it back to before Jesus was born, when persons we
considered not as well informed as we walked in darkness. Right now, darkness over this world that is
caused by sin, poverty and ignorance, is perhaps
blacker than at any previous time. What does it mean
to dwell in the land of the shadow of death?

Think for a moment of people who live near you.
Perhaps they have chosen lifestyles that put them in
perilous situations. Night after night, security guards
at hospital emergency rooms have to evict drug ad-
dicts who have come in hoping for more drugs. These
people continue to live in the shadow of death.

The opposite end of the spectrum is the light that is
Jesus Christ. The darker the place into which the light
comes, the more needed and the more brightly the
Light of the world shines. Jesus came to all who are
in darkness. His very coming, in heavenly light, offers
the only cure for the black night.

I need Your light in my life right now, Lord; bless me with its beams.

> *Those who are wise shall shine like the brightness*
> *of the firmament, and those who turn many to*
> *righteousness like the stars forever and ever.*
> —DAN. 12:3

Each April Fool's day, I (John) get the privilege of trying to track down a friend who is a shining star in my life—not a literal one but the type mentioned in the verse. He was the type of person who was filled with wisdom and shone with God's truth. Because of his faithfulness in sharing the Gospel, both my brothers, my mother, and I came to know Christ; along with many other friends!

This particular shining star is a man named Doug Barram. Then a Young Life Area Director in Phoenix, Doug is now a leader in the "Fellowship," a Christian men's organization.

Doug loved me and many others on my high school campus when he didn't have to. He patiently answered endless questions and shared his wisdom and insight freely. But most of all, he faithfully shared the gospel and challenged many of us to respond who had never been in a church to hear it.

Is there a "shining star" in your life that you could write a note of encouragement to? You may not have the reminder that I do every April Fool's day (Doug's birthday), but your words will be welcome whenever they come to your spiritual mother or father.

Lord, thank You for those whose lights point others toward You.

*"Then the righteous will shine forth as the sun in
the kingdom of their Father."*   —MATT. 13:43

When we really read this verse and consider its
meaning, we cannot help being filled with awe and
wonder. We recognize the power of the sun, a force so
brilliant and overpowering we can't look at it without
special eye protection.

It's hard to imagine that those who serve the Lord
in righteousness will someday be as dazzling as the
sun, yet that is what Jesus promised. This is one of the
blessings and rewards that come to those who endure.

A ninety-five-year-old lady lay in the hospital await-
ing major, high-risk surgery. She said to her family,
"Now, I don't want any of you to worry. I'm not wor-
ried. The Lord is watching over us all."

The blood pressure monitor confirmed her tranquility long before she received medication. This woman's
righteous life made her shine as the sun, a witness to
the entire hospital. She came through the surgery far
better than most people much younger and continued
to tell her nurses and doctors why!

*God, may my ingrained faith shine forth in the toughest situations
and influence those around me.*

> *The light of the gospel of the glory of Christ, who is*
> *the image of God, should shine on them.*
>   —2 COR. 4:4

Several years ago, there was a best-selling song titled, "You light up my life." Like many popular songs before it, it speaks of that special gleam and glow that comes from being in love.

In a home, we are particularly likely to glow when we see a loved one after a long absence. If we're really glad to see them, our eyes will often shine. Proverbs puts it this way, "Bright eyes gladden the heart!"

In today's verse, we are reminded that the gospel of Christ shines with its own light—the light of salvation that cuts through the darkness and opens our lives to God's redeeming light.

Light brings warmth, dispels shadows, causes curtains to be pulled back. God's redeeming light causes healing, restoration, forgiveness, and spiritual repair.

What a blessing that God's light, the very light of heaven, will shine on us one day in all its dazzling splendor!

I need that light in my life so I can reflect to others, Lord.

And your life would be brighter than noonday.
—JOB 11:17

The country in which Job lived, the land of Uz, was familiar with bright noonday sun. So when one of Job's so-called comforter friends, Zophar, set about to chide Job for his shortcomings, he chose the sun as his example.

Something to keep in mind is this. The noonday sun is often spoken of as a sun that casts no shadows. Noon is viewed as the time when the sun sits directly overhead and chases away shade.

Wouldn't it be wonderful if our lives held no shadows? No dark corners or shady places that conceal secret sins, misery, or doubt? Zophar literally promises this—if Job would repent of the iniquity his friend suspected him of hiding.

Job was not hiding sin, as we know from studying the record of his life. He could stand in the noonday sun and not be afraid of the light.

God wants us to be able to do just that: to stand forth, unconcealed, under His penetrating gaze, even though His searchlight is more illuminating than the noonday sun.

Father, remove anything from my life that cannot stand shadowless before Your Son.

*Stand still and consider the wondrous works of
God. Do you know when God dispatches them,
and causes the light of His cloud to shine?*
—JOB 37:14, 15

Our fascination with the sky and clouds is neverending. What child, or adult, hasn't gazed into the clouds at dragons and dogs, mountains and monsters?

This scripture in Job reminds us that even when we see and consider God's wondrous works, we don't know when He dispatches them. Or when He causes light to break through.

Sometimes on an overcast day, a ray of light zeroes in and a shaft pierces the clouds, shimmering with dust motes. We stop to watch and rejoice, for that single beam brings hope of more light coming soon to dispel the clouds.

Perhaps you are surrounded with clouds just now, waiting for that illuminating beam. Take heart, it will come.

Oh God, pierce the clouds with Your light and increase my hope.

*He comes from the north as golden splendor; with
God is awesome majesty.*　　　　　—JOB 37:22

The word *splendor* paints pictures of purple shadows
on red rock canyons and mighty mountains lifting
their heads to their Maker. We might also think of
kings and queens on glittering thrones, wearing lus-
trous jewels and costly clothing.

Majesty enforces our image of royalty, power, and
riches—and, perhaps, someone bowing in adoration of
such glory.

Not all majesty is holy. Writers of fairy tales recognized this. Remember the wicked queens? They had
such splendor and power, they demanded and received service from their minions. The *Alice in Won-
derland* queen made sure her subjects paid her
homage with her, "Off with their heads!" attitude.

God is so far above any earthly splendor, any majes-
tic worldly throne, it's difficult to even find a good
comparison. "Golden splendor" is probably one of the
best, along with "awesome majesty." Sometimes we
get so busy seeing God as "Friend" and "Companion"
(which He certainly is), we lose sight of His majesty.

Fill me with a renewed sense of awe at Your majesty, O God.

*Make Your face shine upon Your servant; save me
for Your mercies' sake.*   —PS. 31:16

Many of the praise verses in the Bible are quite similar, especially those asking for God's face to shine
upon us. This is to be expected. We know that when
we are the receivers of God's smile, good things happen. God's shining face indeed does save us for His
mercy is great and endless. In turn, we need to pass
on smiles to those who have lost theirs.

When someone smiles at us, we feel that we may
have won their friendship, respect, or approval, if the
smile is clearly genuine. Now and then a person shares
how a child's happy smile, a or stranger's, changed a
life bent on destruction.

Isaac Watts wrote a poem more than 200 years ago
that later was set to music. In the fourth stanza of
"Praise Ye the Lord," Watts wrote, "He makes the grass
the hills adorn / And clothes the smiling fields with
corn . . ."

We know that the grass and the corn in those smiling fields take their strength and nurture from the sunshine of God.

_____

Thank You for Your sunshine upon me, Lord, and for Your mercy.

*[Make Your] . . . face to shine upon us, . . . that
Your way may be known, . . . Your salvation
among all nations.* —PS. 67:1

God's face shining on us paves the way for the nations to know God's ways and His salvation.

Recent magazine articles have covered the explosion of revivals in China and other oppressed countries. Let's see how God could have done this.

God could have sent angels to destroy the wicked and pave the path for missionaries to flock in and spread His word. Instead, he allows the faithful to suffer, sometimes even death, in presenting the gospel. We don't know His reasoning. It could be that that which is hardest won becomes our greatest treasure.

Do you know a missionary from your church you could write a blessing letter to today? If not, call for a name!

Bless me today with deeper devotion to You and Your work, Lord.

A man's wisdom makes his face shine.
—ECCL. 8:1

If it has been a while since you watched a child do homework, you may have missed an object lesson that underscores the words of the Preacher.

Danny is a good example. He's great at math and science, but struggles with language arts. Night after night, Danny sat at the dining room table composing not-so-wonderful themes. Usually his upper teeth were holding his bottom lip. His hand on the always-dull pencil was tight.

Not long ago, Danny's hard work paid off. He began to really understand the basic principles his teacher had tried to teach. Wisdom set in like a warm spring breeze. What a difference! Just as the passage said that wisdom makes man's face shine, Danny's new knowledge relaxed his hand and body—and made his face shine.

You may be on a job or in a home situation that is keeping you as tense and upset as Danny has been until very recently. God can give you wisdom that will make your face shine. Ask Him.

Lord, I need Your wisdom, that I may be wise.

"Now therefore, our God, hear the prayer of Your servant, and his supplications, and for the Lord's sake cause Your face to shine on Your sanctuary, which is desolate."
—DAN. 9:17

A young minister, just out of seminary, viewed his first pastorate with dismay. The sad little church bravely lifted its spire toward heaven but the untidy grounds testified to the congregation's discouragement.

Bob remembered his superior's question, "Where do you most want to go to serve?"

Without hesitation, Bob had replied, "Where I am needed most."

Well, if ever a church needed help it had to be this one!

Bob found lodging nearby. Early Monday morning he sought his Lord in prayer and the words of Daniel became his watchword. Instead of calling or visiting the few church members, Bob borrowed tools from his landlord and set to work. By night, the lawn was weedless and the flowers had perked up. The next days sped by in a flurry of scraping and sanding the church building. On Friday, some of the faithful "dropped by" in work clothes.

On Sunday morning, a small group met in a newly painted church that had been swept clean of both dust and desolation. God surely smiled—and the church grew.

Lord, shine Your face on my church. May we each know Your presence.

September

THE LORD BE GRACIOUS TO YOU

Grace and peace be multiplied to you in the knowledge of God and of Jesus our Lord.
—2 PETER 1:2

The month of September is a month of change in many places. School begins in a month of still-hot days and cool nights.

September is a graceful month, a transitional time. It's a good time to reflect on the graciousness of God. How fitting to begin with this verse. Children the world over are learning multiplication tables.

Peter pronounces a beautiful blessing to the saints of his time, "Grace and peace be multiplied to you in the knowledge of God and of Jesus our Lord." This is a blessing we can give to ourselves and to others. It is a blessing we can receive when we embark on a new program of study. If you are not already doing so, consider beginning a regular Bible study and prayer time. Watch yourself grow.

Thank You, Lord, for new beginnings.

> *His divine power has given to us all things*
> *that pertain to life and godliness, through*
> *the knowledge of Him who called us by*
> *glory and virtue.* —2 PETER 1:3

The great Roman historian Livy (Titus Livius) wrote, "Men are slower to recognize blessings than evils." Our attitudes today confirm this. We typically say, "I hit every red light in town on my way here," more often than, "I hit all green lights." Or, instead of recognizing God's many protective blessings, we ask, "God, why didn't You step in and protect me?"

Recall as many important things from yesterday as you can. Look past the ones that are not good. Consider your blessings, no matter how small. Now, thank God for these minute favors—and keep your heart open today for knowledge of more blessings.

You give us all we need, Lord, and for this I praise Your name.

[He has] given to us exceedingly great and precious promises.
— 2 PETER 1:4

The new third grade teacher simply could not control her students. Afraid she would lose her job, she changed tactics. "If you are all good and do your work well," she promised, "I will take our whole class to Disneyland next summer, when school's out."

The excited children told their parents, who flocked to school to see what was going on. No young teacher could afford to keep such an exceedingly great promise, no matter how precious to the students. As soon as the administration could get a replacement, the foolish teacher was replaced by a woman who never made a promise she couldn't keep.

Peter wasn't satisfied to say that God's promises are great and precious, but added the word *exceedingly.* This is the man who walked and talked with Jesus, who loved and betrayed Him, who rose above the agony of remembrance when forgiven and served his risen Lord. He has the authority to know.

Lord, may I lean more fully on Your great and precious promises.

But also for this very reason [being partakers of the divine nature and escaping worldly corruption], giving all diligence, . . . —2 PETER 1:5

This verse begins another list of qualities God desires us to seek and develop. Today, the word *diligence* offers guidelines to God's high expectations of us.

What are the qualities of a diligent person? One who practices diligence might be alert, constant, industrious, and careful.

If you'd like a living example of diligence, drive past an elementary school when it's letting out for the day. Observe the traffic guard. Check out how alert, constant, and careful the guard is.

We as Christians ought to learn from the traffic guards. They guard young lives; we are commissioned as guardians of human souls. All the attributes that make a traffic guard a good servant of the school are necessary for us to be good servants of our Master. He will bless us to this end.

Lord, may I have diligence in following Your commands.

Add to your faith.
—2 PETER 1:5

The eternal truths that make a hymn written more than a hundred years earlier relevant to our times are exquisitely expressed in Ray Palmer's, "My Faith Looks Up to Thee."

> *My faith looks up to thee, Thou Lamb of Calvary,*
> *Savior divine!*
> *Now hear me while I pray, Take all my guilt away;*
> *Oh, let me from this day be wholly thine!*
> *May thy rich grace impart Strength to my fainting*
> *heart, . . .*
> *While life's dark maze I tread, And griefs around*
> *me spread,*
> *Be thou my guide . . .*

A meaningful pattern is given in this heartfelt prayer. First, a statement of needing the Savior followed by repentance and forgiveness. Next comes recognition of the great need sinners have for strength and guidance. Palmer ends with a petition that wandering feet and hearts may be kept firm and steady.

These blessings are the ones that come through faith.

———————

Increase my faith, impart strength, guide my feet, O Lord.

> *Add to your faith virtue.*
> —2 PETER 1:5

Emily Dickinson wrote this verse:

> *We never know how high we*
> *are*
> *Till we are called to rise;*
> *And then, if we are true to plan,*
> *Our statures touch the skies.*

This is certainly true of a virtuous person. It is also interesting how much insight the poet showed into human nature for she lived in seclusion, seeing only a few close friends.

There are times we need to back away from our world and contemplate its meaning. Most of us don't have the time or freedom to retreat into seclusion to just think. Yet if we are to acquire virtue, time for considering God's truths is mandatory.

In Emily Dickinson's poem is expressed the paradox of life. None of us can know our degree of virtue. God alone reserves the right to examine the human heart. The poem does offer a clue, however, in the words "if we are true to plan." The Master's plan is for every person to be filled with His virtue.

_____

Help me to strive toward the virtue embodied in Your Son, Lord.

To virtue [add] knowledge.
—2 PETER 1:5

In classrooms across the nation and across the world, students are studying with bent heads and at least some degree of concentration.

There are other resources from which we can obtain knowledge necessary to live successfully. The most important is the Bible, with its teachings for a complete life.

An unknown author offers thought-provoking words.

THE ANVIL—GOD'S WORD

Last eve I passed beside a blacksmith's door,
And heard the anvil ring the vesper chime;
Then, looking in, I saw upon the floor
Old hammers, worn with beating years of time.

"How many anvils have you had," said I,
"To wear and batter all these hammers so?"
"Just one," said he, and then, with twinkling eye,
"The anvil wears the hammers out, you know."

And so, thought I, the anvil of God's Word,
For ages skeptic blows have beat upon;
Yet, though the noise of falling blows was heard,
The anvil is unharmed—the hammers gone.

True knowledge is that which outlasts all the attempts to disprove it. We are blessed because of its stability.

May I cherish most the knowledge of You, Lord, my anvil.

To knowledge [add] self-control.
—2 PETER 1:6

Mighty machines have built-in checks and balances that keep them performing as they were meant to perform. Yet occasionally, something deep inside goes haywire. The results can be devastating unless help is obtained quickly.

We also have built-in checks and balances, designed and placed by our Heavenly Father to help us be in control. But, just as the machines go out of control, so do human lives. What occurs then is even more devastating than a machine going wild.

A few weeks ago we looked at self-control as one of the fruits of the Spirit. Here, we see Peter advising the early saints to work on developing self-control, along with faith and virtue and knowledge.

But what is self-control? The Greek word for *self-control* means, "To pull in the reigns." In other words, like a runaway horse, we don't let any emotion or appetite run anywhere it wants. We exhibit control or "keep the reins pulled in" on habits and attitudes that may be destructive.

Thank You, Lord, that You can give me the strength to "pull in the reins" when I need to.

To self-control [add] perseverance.
—2 PETER 1:6

Some people feel they just don't have any perseverance. They're probably right. When faced with new situations, they may try once and, if they fail, that's it.

For a real blessing, look to children as a source of inspiration. There is a direct correlation between perseverance and motivation. A student may study into the wee hours to get good grades. A tennis player may intensely pursue his sport. The energy and will to achieve in a given area will provide the perseverance to win.

People who have been informed they will never walk or run again have persevered in agonizing exercises until they disproved the medical experts. We say they have winners' hearts.

What do you need to persevere in today?

I know You want me to be a winner, Lord; help me to increase my perseverance.

> *To perseverance [add] godliness.*
> —2 PETER 1:6

Before we can stretch on tiptoe to grow in godliness, we must know what it means. What are the characteristics of God? Let's look at a few of the obvious traits He wants us to possess. God is loving, just, consistent, concerned, compassionate, caring, and always available.

Suppose we made these traits part of our lives. Can you imagine what a difference it would make to us, to our families, to our acquaintances and friends—our society?

For example, we would have no fear of the law as we would live above it. There is a forty-mile speed limit near Edward's property. His neighbors grumble about it and ignore it. They also speed and receive tickets.

Edward doesn't worry about getting ticketed. From the time the speed limit took effect, he has determined to never exceed it. By living above the law, he has freedom.

Father, may I practice godliness in all areas of my life.

To godliness [add] brotherly kindness.
—2 PETER 1:7

During Civil War days, one of the greatest fears was that of meeting a relative in combat. It wasn't uncommon for one brother to be fighting for the Union and another for the Confederacy. The concepts of brotherly kindness, preached and taught in Christian homes, took on new meaning.

When the devastation and destruction ended and those soldiers who escaped death came home, the war of hatred and resentment still raged in many hearts. In other cases, families and neighbors were wise enough to realize they must bury the past along with their dead and face a new era.

A pleasant sight is to see brothers who haven't seen each other for a long time. They slap each other on the back and some joke around to hide their emotion, but in their eyes you can see brotherly kindness.

This brotherly kindness can be evidenced in all our lives—not only toward family and friends, but toward strangers and those in need.

As Your Son blessed me with brotherly kindness, Lord, may I share it with others.

To brotherly kindness [add] love.
—2 PETER 1:7

Saint Augustine wrote, "God loves each one of us, as if there was only one of us." In the times we feel of little value and need a blessing of self-worth, these words ring in our hearts and lift our spirits. We are special parts of His creation, of equal value in His sight. Our Father would that we might accept His patient, everlasting love and make it part of our own lives. Because of God's love, we are rich in blessings and the promise of eternal life with Him.

During our lives, we experience many kinds of love, both as givers and receivers. The shallow admiration of "I love ice cream" comments has little to do with the love we know when a man and woman join before God in marriage or a new saint from darkness into light.

Uplift my love, Lord, until all of it is acceptable to Thee.

Then he [Joseph] . . . saw his brother Benjamin, . . .
and said, . . . "God be gracious to you, my son."
—GEN. 43:29

Long years had passed since Joseph's older brothers tired of him being their father's favorite. Disgusted with Joseph's dreams that showed his mother, father and brothers bowing down to him, the brothers had sold him to the Ishmaelites, who took him to Egypt. He was sold to Potiphar, and served as his overseer—until Potiphar's false wife landed Joseph a prison term. Joseph left prison to interpret Pharaoh's dream.

When Joseph advised storing up food against the coming famine, Pharaoh made Joseph second-in-command of the land.

Imagine Joseph's brothers' surprise when they realized who Joseph was. But Joseph could scarcely contain himself when he saw his brother Benjamin. He pronounced this beautiful blessing on Benjamin and praised God for the crooked path that had allowed him to be in a position to save his starving family.

"God be gracious to you, my son," blesses both speaker and hearer.

God, help me be faithful in speaking words of blessing.

> *"It will be that when he [your neighbor] cries to Me,
> I will hear, for I am gracious."* —EX. 22:27

In this paragraph, the people are warned that if they take a neighbor's garment as a pledge, it must be returned before sundown so the man will have something to sleep in. Why? Because God hears the neighbor's cry; He is gracious.

We of the twentieth century don't take our neighbor's garments for pledges; however, there are some situations we can compare to that custom.

What would God say to the owner of the only clothing store, in a poverty-stricken area, who raises prices until the people can't afford to clothe their children? God still hears our neighbors' cries.

Bless me with the determination to help right this world's wrongs by using the graciousness You have given me.

> *"I will be gracious to whom I will be gracious, and I will have compassion on whom I will have compassion."*
> —EX. 33:19

It is easy to wonder about God's ways when they don't conform to the way we see things. Many times we ask, "Why are such terrible things happening to such a devoted Christian family? They've served God all their lives. Now, everything is falling apart. Why, God?"

We cannot understand why God apparently pours blessings out on one deserving family and seemingly turns His face from another, equally worthy.

To us comes the startling pronouncement from Exodus. God chooses those to whom He will be gracious and He has compassion on those He chooses. Period. There may be a hundred unseen factors only God knows. He has the right to choose when and how He will show graciousness and compassion. It all fits in His master plan. We don't have to understand; we just need to trust Him.

Lord, I don't always understand Your plan, but I do want to trust You.

> *According to the grace of God which was given to me, . . . I have laid the foundation, and another builds on it.*
> —1 COR. 3:10

Years ago when a man wanted a home, he either built it himself or hired the village carpenter. Now, when we watch the construction of developments, we see teams of workers, each with their own specialties.

What a joy to build a foundation of God's love and the plan of salvation in a friend's life and see the acceptance. It is an equal blessing to know another will build.

As with many of Paul's writings, this verse contains a lot of depth that may not surface until we read and reread the words.

First, he recognized his Source. He acknowledged that God's grace was a gift, not a prize or payment. Paul concluded with the matter-of-fact acceptance that he wouldn't necessarily be the builder, once he had laid the foundation.

Lord, help me to remember I need not always see the results of the work I do for You.

Gracious is the Lord, and righteous.
—PS. 116:5

It wasn't necessary to tell the world that God is both gracious and righteous. Yet David proclaimed it, again and again. Because God had done so much for him and brought him through many trials and temptations, David simply couldn't keep silent.

Can you remember a time when God, in His grace and righteousness, blessed you abundantly? Chances are, you couldn't wait to tell everyone who would listen.

Andraé Crouch's beautiful song, "My Tribute," expresses well how impossible it is to adequately express our thanks to God and to give Him the praise and glory due Him. Mr. Crouch concluded that we must simply acknowledge that everything we are and may become is due to God's grace.

The psalmist's reminder of God's righteousness is also a reminder of our goal to grow more like His Son. What better pursuit in life can we have than that of righteousness and His blessings?

Father, that my life would be a tribute to You, is my prayer.

> "*Who can tell whether the Lord will be gracious to me . . . ?*"
> —2 SAM. 12:22

To paraphrase this portion of Scripture, who can tell *when* the Lord is gracious to us?

Obvious blessings, such as receiving those things we pray for, may be seen as evidence that the Lord has shown graciousness to us. However, when He answers according to His best plan and not our pre-set agenda, we may not recognize or accept His graciousness.

An old, rather unfamiliar song spoke of yet unanswered prayers. It assured the burden bearers that sometime, somewhere, God would answer. It is comforting to know that not one prayer goes unheard or is lost in God's incoming-calls file.

Prayer is two-sided. When we earnestly call on God for someone else, the blessings *we* receive are great. Although we may rise from our knees still carrying at least part of the burden, prayer is what strengthens us to rise and go on.

Years after God responds to our prayers differently than we had hoped, we may see His true graciousness in not granting our request.

Whatever blessing comes from You is the right one, Father.

*Yet for many years you had patience with
them, . . . For You are God, gracious and merciful.*
—NEH. 9:30, 31

I am losing my patience," a kindergarten teacher
warned her restless students. "And when this happens,
we don't have a happy class."

The teacher reflects all of us. When patience is exhausted, our environment takes on a miserable atmosphere.

At the beginning of Nehemiah's story, he has discovered that the wall of Jerusalem is broken and its gates
are burned down. He weeps, fasts, mourns and prays.
Then he gets permission from King Artaxerxes to go
to Judah and rebuild the wall.

When he and his company rejoined their brethren
in Jerusalem, the children of Israel assembled with
fasting, sackclock and ashes. They repented, confessed their sins, and worshipped the Lord. They gave
thanks and acknowledged God's patience with the
people who had disobeyed His laws.

*Lord, You are so patient with me. Thank You for Your gracious
mercy.*

> *The fear of the Lord is the beginning of wisdom,*
> *And the knowledge of the Holy One is*
> *understanding.*　　　　　　　　　　—PROV. 9:10

What does fear have to do with wisdom?

Several years ago, I (John) took up mountain-biking. In the desert where I live, there is a mountain preserve with numerous trails to ride. One early winter morning, as I was coming down a narrow trail, I passed right by a huge rattlesnake stretched straight as an arrow.

I know there were snakes around, but I'd never taken time to learn much about them. I stopped my bike, thinking that the snake must be dead and started to walk back toward it. But as I reached out to pick it up, it raised its tail and slowly began to crawl off the trail.

I'd nearly picked up a live, four foot rattlesnake— which suddenly seemed ten feet long! It wasn't dead, just sunning itself. Talk about fear! And talk about being more teachable thereafter.

Fear became a powerful motivator for me to learn more about the animals I was sharing the mountain preserve with.

Realizing God's power, might, and majesty can cause us to tremble with positive fear—but not the paralyzing fear of picking up a snake but the type of fear and respect that causes us to want to love and serve Him becauses He's the King of Kings!

Thank You, Lord, for Your power and majesty that can motivate us to love and serve You.

As newborn babes, desire the pure milk of the word, that you may grow thereby, if indeed you have tasted that the Lord is gracious.
—1 PETER 2:2, 3

Peter describes the word of the Lord in an unusual way here. He goes on to say that once God's graciousness has been tasted, then desire should be fanned for the pure milk of the Word.

Recent studies continue to confirm how important mother's milk is to the development of their babies. Children, teens, and athletes drink milk to strengthen their bodies. Although some people can't tolerate milk there are many ways to get the needed nourishment.

Setting time aside for the pure milk of the word can be in a variety of ways, as well.

Help me to never get enough of the pure milk of Your word, Father.

> *O Lord, be gracious to us;*
> *We have waited for You.*
> —ISA. 33:2

For Kenneth and Karen, the worst "waiting" experience they ever had was waiting outside the judge's chambers while he decided who would be awarded custody of Kenneth's daughter—Kenneth or his ex-wife. For seven-year-old Tim, waiting for summer vacation is the hardest "wait" he's ever experienced. Tim's seventeen-year-old brother, on the other hand, "can't wait" to get a car.

Waiting for God is as difficult as waiting for promised things to come or for stress to end. Isaiah implores God to be gracious because the people have waited for Him.

Yet, is the wait worth it? Absolutely!

Teach me God, to wait—not just on You, but for You.

*Therefore comfort each other and edify one
another, just as you also are doing.*
—1 THESS. 5:11

Moms and Dads, I wish there were some way I could
communicate to you the incredible blessing of affirming words. I wish, too, that I could have you sit in my
office when I counsel and hear the terrible damage
suffered from not hearing them.

If affirming words were rarely spoken in your home,
let me give you some tips on words and phrases that
can brighten a child's eyes and life. These words are
easy to say to *any child* that comes into your life this
month and may make all the difference in a little heart.

• I'm proud of you • Way to go • Bingo . . . you did it • Magnificent • I knew you could do it • What a good helper •
You're very special to me • I trust you • What a treasure •
Hurray for you • Beautiful work • You're a real trooper •
Well done • That's so creative • You make my day • You're
a joy • Give me a big hug • You're such a good listener •
You figured it out • I love you • You're so responsible • You
remembered • You're the best • You sure tried hard • I've
got to hand it to you • I couldn't be prouder of you • You
light up my day • I'm praying for you • You're wonderful
• I'm behind you • You're so kind to your (brother/sister)
• You're God's special gift • I'm here for you •

---

*Lord, let me go on the offensive this month when it comes to affirm-
ing and valuing my loved ones.*

> *Return to the Lord, your God, for He is . . . slow to*
> *anger, and of great kindness.*   —JOEL 2:13

According to legend, the ancient Greek philosopher, Diogenes, walked the streets with a lantern held high, searching for an honest man. Whether he ever found one is unknown.

Suppose for a moment that you are a modern Diogenes, only instead of seeking an honest man, you look for a kind person. Joel says God is of great kindness. It's reasonable to suppose that His followers should evidence the same type of behavior.

You won't need a lantern in your search. You will need sharp eyes and ears. The truly kind people don't brag about it. Consider the tired schoolteacher who, in the evenings, helps immigrants learn English. How about the mother of four, who keeps an eye on her elderly neighbors.

Now think about the kindness you have received from God and others. Can you name one deed of kindness you performed recently?

Make me kinder today than I have ever been before, God.

They [the Israelites] refused to obey, and they were not mindful of Your wonders. . . . But You are God, ready to pardon, gracious and merciful, . . . and did not forsake them.
—NEH. 9:17

The world watches and waits for a governor's decision. Will he pardon a convicted criminal with a stay of execution or let it stand? The evidence clearly shows the man is guilty. What will the governor do?

The evidence presented in Nehemiah is just as clear. Guilt is written all over the people's faces. It's possible we, today, are just as guilty of rebellion as the long-ago Israelites. The wonderful news is that God not only *will* pardon but that He is *ready* to pardon, again, through his graciousness.

He must have wanted to shake those Israelites when they started whining. Sometimes we echo their cries in times of stress. Yet the blessings that follow those who hold on are many.

I know You will never forsake me, Father; the blessing of this knowledge empowers me.

> *So all bore witness to Him, and marveled at the*
> *gracious words which proceeded out of His mouth.*
> *And they said, "Is this not Joseph's son?"*
> —LUKE 4:22

It is easy to get impatient with people in the New Testament who saw and heard Jesus, yet didn't recognize Him. Most of us pride ourselves that we would surely know Him if we were to meet Him or hear Him teach.

Luke tells of how Jesus read the Scriptures aloud in the synagogue at Nazareth. When He sat down, everyone stared at Him. Then, Jesus pronounced words far beyond his listeners' understanding and told them the Scripture had just been fulfilled.

First, the people marveled at the gracious way Jesus spoke. The contrast between the power and authority of Jesus' words compared to most readers must have been great. But then, whispers hissed throughout the synagogue. The blessing that allowed them to at first discern and marvel at His words dissipated before their doubt.

Do you need to be blessed that you might marvel at God's words?

Father, help me to discern Your voice and not to doubt.

A man who isolates himself seeks his own desire;
He rages against all wise judgment.
—PROV. 18:1

How would you like to increase your lifespan and decrease your susceptibility to sickness? Sound like a sales pitch? It is . . . for the wisdom this verse preaches.

People who isolate themselves are making a major mistake. A recent study was done with a group of widows whose spouses had died by either suicide or accident. One year after the deaths of their partners, the widows were asked to indicate how they had responded to what happened, as well as to list the health problems they had encountered during that year. The results were striking.

The more frequently the subjects discussed their spouse's death with other people—particularly in a supportive context of a small group—the fewer the health problems they experienced. The more they brooded alone about the death, not discussing it with others, the more and greater their health problems.

Other studies show that even the common cold strikes those in small groups less often than it does those who don't have such a support. Perhaps, this is why people who attend church are in better overall health—and live longer—than those who do not.

All these statistics and studies point to one thing: biblical truth. It's important that we don't isolate ourselves from others.

Lord, help me to not forsake gathering, loving and sharing with others.

> *"Then he is gracious to him, and says, 'Deliver him from going down to the Pit; I have found a ransom.'"*
>
> —JOB 33:24

The height of graciousness that the Lord shows us is in the life, death, and resurrection of Jesus Christ as our ransom. He paid the price that we might also live, then die, and be resurrected whole and sinless.

Perhaps nothing on earth is any more terrifying than to discover a family member is missing. In kidnapping cases, families cling to the phone, waiting, yet dreading the time it will ring. If only a ransom demand would come, perhaps there would be a moment of hearing the loved one's voice. Even when the ransom call or note comes, the terror isn't over. There is no assurance of restoration, even if the ransom is paid.

When Jesus paid our ransom, He also took away the dreadful fear. We have His promise: all who believe on Him as their Lord and Savior are made whole and are freed from the bonds of captivity. Praise Him for that blessing.

_____

Thank You, Lord, for the ransom paid by Jesus; for my life in You.

"I know that You are a gracious and merciful God,
slow to anger and abundant in lovingkindness, One
who relents from doing harm." —JONAH 4:2

Jonah resisted God. "No way, Lord, am I going to preach to the people in Nineveh." He hopped the first ship and fled. Thus his troubles began. Three days and nights in the Whale Inn made him a wiser man.

Did he learn from his experience? Enough to go preach the way he was instructed and to warn the inhabitants of Nineveh of dire results if they didn't repent. Jonah evidently didn't learn enough compassion, graciousness, or mercy to rejoice when God spared the repentant people.

The phrase, "relents from doing harm," implies that even when destruction is on its way, the wholehearted turnabout of a people can make a difference.

Thank You, God, for your lovingkindness.

> *"But now entreat God's favor, that He may be gracious to us."*
> —MAL. 1:9

The Frank Capra movie *It's a Wonderful Life* continues to win new generations of fans with its simple message that life truly is wonderful. One of the most significant parts of the movie is the beginning. Prayers are shooting skyward on behalf of the distressed, well-loved George Bailey. Those prayers were heard and answered, though not as expected. His friends and family couldn't have dreamed how George Bailey would learn the sacredness of life.

During our lives, we play many roles: the troubled, desperate George Bailey; the spouse or child of someone fighting life battles; a prayerful friend.

Just as in the movie, neither do we know how God will answer our prayers, just that He will—in the best way. He will also be gracious in giving us the strength and courage to accept His divine will. Is that what you need right now? Tell Him.

Loving Father, I ask for Your favor for my loved ones and for myself. Thank You for this blessing.

October

THE LORD LIFT UP HIS COUNTENANCE

> *The Lord is my shepherd.*
> —PS. 23:1

Many beautiful pictures of Christ focus on various parts of his personality. The painting that shows Christ with a lamb in His arms especially appeals to us when we're feeling down and in need of comfort.

Most of us pride ourselves that we can handle whatever life offers. Secretly, we face many times when we appear to be okay, but are falling apart inside. That's the time to concentrate on the Lord as Shepherd. A shepherd takes the responsibility for his flock, protects them, nurtures them and gathers them into his arms.

God also holds us close in times of trouble. He's not like the grandfather so surrounded by grandchildren there isn't room on his lap. There is room in God's arms for every suffering or weary soul. Just as a good shepherd picks up lost lambs and carries them over hard places, so does God carry us.

Perhaps you are experiencing grief or pain, frustration or indecision. Try picturing yourself as caught up into God's arms like the lamb you are. You'll be blessed.

May I feel Your strong arms holding me this day, Good Shepherd.

I shall not want.
—PS. 23:1

There are two distinct definitions of *want*. The usual one is found in our "I want this; I want that" attitudes. The other meaning of *want* is to be without.

It appears David was referring to the second definition, rather than promising that God will give us everything we desire.

Helen Steiner Rice wrote a heartwarming poem based on the legend of "The Windows of Gold." A boy who lived in a mountain cabin looked down into the valley at sunrise and saw beautiful windows. He trekked down the mountain, only to find that the windows were dark and ugly. Then a kindly person pointed at the windows of the boy's cabin, touched by the setting sun, turned into windows of gold. The underlying theme was that the kingdom of God, with all the things that fill our want, is within our own hearts.

Is there an area of your life that is in want, not just wanting things? God is big enough to fill it.

God, show me my own windows of gold by enlarging my soul.

He makes me to lie down in green pastures.
—PS. 23:2

All day the Navajo herdsman had driven his employer's sheep, from the high desert plateau down the autumn-touched slopes, back to the home range. Footsore and weary, the plodding man kept the animals moving. They wouldn't remember what lay ahead but the Navajo knew and was glad.

It would be good to winter in the canyon where plenty of water spread a green, soft carpet of fields and pastures before them.

When they reached the ranch, the shepherd led the sheep through the gate into the large, enclosed area. Good grass swished about his ankles. The sheep browsed, then lay down to rest. And the herdsman smiled.

Many can't now understand how much significance lies in the simple statement, "He makes me to lie down in green pastures." We can wonder, how dangerous or frightening was the way to the green pastures? How scratched and bruised were the sheep when they arrived?

Our own green pastures of blessing can be found in God's love.

The blessing of rest in peaceful, green pastures is invaluable.

He leads me beside the still waters.
—PS. 23:2

White water rafting and salmon fishing are two of my family's (John's) favorite activities. However, we wouldn't choose a turbulent or noisy body of water beside which to camp when we need to be refreshed in mind or spirit. Rushing water is for stimulation; still waters for rest.

If you want a real experience in tranquility, take a few days off and find a place beside still waters, where only the frogs croaking or the fish splashing can distract you.

David was grateful to God for leading him beside still waters. We need the same experience, if we are to keep our perspective. Much of our time rushes by like the river, eager to reach the sea. We must have still-water times if we are to stay close to our Heavenly Father and carry on.

I need still waters in my life, Lord; thank You for blessing me.

He restores my soul.
—PS. 23:3

Persons interested in antiques may spend many hours restoring something worn, even ugly, to its original luster and beauty.

Restoration cannot be done unless that object or person had something "stored up" in the first place. Who knows what is under years' accumulation of paint, or what treasure will be found under a dirt crust?

Our souls are our greatest treasures. So when David wrote that God restores his soul, he was telling us that the Lord had vision enough to see beyond his crusted-over veneer, reach into his heart, and get rid of the junk. Only in so doing can the real worth that once shone brighter than light itself again be seen.

The blessing of being restored comes from God. We can, however, help restore others.

Lord, is there one this day I can help restore to You?

He leads me in the paths of righteousness for His
name's sake.   —PS. 23:3

The message of Psalms is that God lives, works in our lives, and is interested in every aspect of life. Here we see that God leads us in the paths of righteousness— for His name's sake.

Let's examine the position in which David found himself when he repented of his wicked ways and again set his face toward God. All Israel had been buzzing about his sin with Bathsheba. The gossip must have grown louder and louder when David took his stand for the Lord. Wasn't this the same king who had acted so abominably? Now here he was singing the praises of God and warning others day and night. Was the fervent prayer and the new attitude permanent, or a passing whim?

To uphold the honor and dignity of God's name, David needed to walk in the paths of righteousness. Anyone who claims to be a follower of the Master but chooses the path of destruction casts a slur on His name. Conversely, those who stand tall and strong and live righteously enhance God's name among the people.

Bless me and lead me in Your righteous path today, O Lord.

> *Yea, though I walk through the valley of the*
> *shadow of death, I will fear no evil.* —PS. 23:4

Death perches on hospital roofs, prepared to take his toll, wearing two faces. To those left behind, death seems cruel, sometimes senseless, and is often misunderstood.

Death is also kindly. Death ends suffering and is the gate through which we must all pass to meet our Heavenly Father. David recognizes this second face when he knows that there is no need to fear the valley of the shadow of death or to view it as evil.

Henry Wadsworth Longfellow wrote, "Look not mournfully into the Past. It comes not back again. Wisely improve the Present. It is thine. Go forth to meet the shadowy future, without fear, and with a manly heart."

Children are often afraid of shadows. Ever-moving, shifting, changing, it is easy to imagine frightening things in their midst. Do you have a shadow in your life that frightens you?

God, bring me out of the shadows into the clear light of Your loving care.

I will fear no evil; for You are with me.
—PS. 23:4

Tad often walked home from basketball practice in the dark. The neighborhood took on a whole new look. Familiar landmarks grew eerie. Daytime-friendly dogs growled and crouched to protect their homes when Tad passed by. The boy usually quickened his tired steps and reached his home almost running.

When a new family moved in a few houses away and Tad discovered Joe meant to go out for basketball, he rejoiced. No more walking home alone through the dark. No more feeling angry because he was scared. The first night they walked home together, Joe said, "Neat neighborhood."

Tad glanced around at the streetlights, no longer lurking figures, and at the dogs who growled only until they recognized him. All fear of evil had fled. "Yeah, it is."

We need a friend to walk beside us when the way is dark or lonely or scary. Jesus is that Friend. He makes the difference between a frightening life and a neat, secure one.

Thank You, Lord, for Your Son and His companionship; I am blessed.

You are with me; Your rod and Your staff, they
comfort me. —PS. 23:4

It's always good to gain extra insight into the objects used by biblical writers to show the correlation between the physical and the spiritual.

The rod and staff were familiar tools of a shepherd. A rod could be described as a short, heavy club with which the shepherd could beat off threatening animals. The staff was for a different purpose. Long and with a crook at one end, the shepherd used it to pull a sheep or lamb back from danger or out of a thicket.

David took comfort in God's rod and staff. With them, the Father drove away Satan and drew David back from life's dangers.

If you ever drive through western states, you may see flocks of sheep being tended by shepherds much as they have always been cared for. How much more consistent is God's continuing care of His sheep.

Great comfort is ours, O Lord; truly we are blessed.

You prepare a table before me in the presence of my enemies.
                                              —PS. 23:5

In the old adventure movies, the hero was often shown walking into a bar full of "bad guys," strolling past them as their countenances bristled, and sitting down and eating with no apparent qualm. As children, we *oohed* and *ahhhed* at such dauntless heroism. As adults, we wonder why the hero wasn't on a horse, running for help.

The David who wrote Psalm 23 was the hero David who faced Goliath, armed with a slingshot. David was the hero of the Hebrews, but he was not foolish. He went forth in the name and might of the living God. He knew God fully cared for His own. So he could face his enemies with the small weapon he had.

Sarah sometimes thinks she is in David's situation when she joins the office staff for lunch. Refusing alcoholic beverages leaves her feeling alienated. Sarah has learned that God cares for her and understands her desire to honor Him rather than return to her former lifestyle. And she trusts God will love her through the teasing from the other staff.

Enemies come in many forms, Lord; Your blessings vary to meet, match, and overcome.

> *You anoint my head with oil; my cup runs over.*
> —PS. 23:5

Have you ever noticed that when a cup overflows the liquid doesn't just settle into a puddle under the cup? If there is much of an overflow, it spreads out wider into quite a damp spot.

Christian lives are like that. At the times we are most filled with God's Spirit, we can't help bubbling over. Our enthusiasm and excitement spills over and spreads into a widening circle of friends.

Helen Lowrie Marshall's poem "Thanks Giving" tells how a person tried to pray and thank God but the blessings of that day grew until they couldn't all be crowded into one small prayer.

Then, God's whisper came and reminded the person that the heart had said the prayer.

Words are always inadequate. The deepest gratitude is not expressed by the lips but in the flash of grateful eyes, the fervent clasp of a hand. So is the depth of our soul offered to the God who pours His peace into our hearts until it spills in tears and joy.

May I experience this day, Lord, Your overflowing Spirit.

"But Moses' hands became heavy . . . and Aaron and Hur supported his hands, one on one side, and the other on the other side; and his hands were steady until the going down of the sun."

—EX. 17:12

In a verse about a major battle, we can see a principle that can help us lead victorious lives.

Under the command of Joshua, the arm of Israel fought bravely against the Amalekites. But victory was far from certain.

From his vantage point on top of a hill, Moses saw that as long as he held up the staff of God in his hands, Israel was winning the battle. But when he lowered his hands, the tide turned in favor of the Amalekites. So Moses bravely stood and held up the staff, but his hands became heavy.

Inevitably, his strength would begin to wane, his arm drop slowly, and Israel would be defeated. But that didn't happen because Moses had *support*.

Aaron stood on one side of Moses, helping him hold up one hand. And Hur stood on the other side, supporting his other hand. The result was a great victory for Israel that day.

With all the pressures and trials we face today, it's hard to stand alone. There is power in linking up with a few good friends who can help us become the man or woman God calls us to be.

Thank You, Lord, for examples of support like Aaron and Hur. May I be like them to a friend in my life.

I will dwell in the house of the Lord forever.
—PS. 23:6

It's always fun to go to a friend's new, or new-to-them, home and see what kind of place it is. Houses are individual in style and decor. God's house, as we know it on earth, is also of varied styles and decor.

David's concept of God's house on earth would have been the temple he wanted to build in Jerusalem. But he isn't referring to that. He's thinking ahead, to dwelling for the rest of eternity in a place that all the information given by various Bible writers can't make clear to the human mind. We do know, however, God's house is big enough to welcome every soul who seeks Him and claims salvation through Jesus Christ.

We furnish our homes with many colors. So does God. All shades brighten God's house. We plant flowers. God's blooming flowers never die. We invite family and friends to our home. God invites the world. What's more, we have God's Word that it's waiting for us.

Lord, I look forward to coming home to You. Please bless my earthly home until that day.

*My son, do not forget my law, but let your heart
keep my commands; for length of days and long
life and peace they will add to you.*
                                        —PROV. 3:1–2

All through the Bible we are reminded how important it is to keep God's law and obey His commands. Here, Solomon asserts that doing so brings blessing, length of days, long life, peace.

Most of us are privileged to know some elderly Christian man or woman whose life embodies this promise. Perhaps since early childhood she has served her Lord. Maybe he came to Christ in middle age and worked hard to make up for the wasted years apart from his Savior. Their work-worn lives and hands may tremble, but the offering of radiance and peace is precious.

If only every person knew this scripture and lived accordingly, he would know: *length of days,* more days in which to serve Him; *long life,* to be enjoyed with His children; and *peace,* one of the greatest gifts a heart can have.

Are you looking forward to or already enjoying these blessings? _____

May I be faithful to keep Your commands, Lord!

> *A merry heart makes a cheerful countenance.*
> —PROV. 15:13

Smiles and laughter begin in the heart and soul. People smile amidst trouble, but according to Solomon, a truly cheerful face comes from a merry heart.

One thing that allows a heart to be merry is contentment. Consider times when you have felt contented and at peace with yourself and the world. Now think of your discontented times. How easy was it to be merry when you were longing for a better job, for your spouse to change, for more money or a better home, or for more disciplined children?

Discontent can be positive. If we never felt dissatisfied with anything, we'd settle for status quo or less. Sometimes God plants a divine discontent in us to prod us into action.

Lord, may my heart be merry, my countenance cheerful.

In the light of the king's face is life.
—PROV. 16:15

Court jesters didn't have it so good. They worked long and unpredictable hours. Whenever the king felt grumpy or discouraged, he summoned the court jester.

"Amuse me," the king would order.

The best and wisest jesters didn't rely on just one trick or form of entertainment. They kept music, dance, magic tricks, jokes, etc. in their repertoire. A bored king could be a dangerous king. The royal frown threatened an "Off with his head" order.

If the king laughed and his face grew light, the jester surely must have leaped even higher and turned better cartwheels, *for the light of the king's face meant life.*

People who saw Christ glorified at the Transfiguration, and again at the Resurrection, spoke of the light in His face. That light offers life to all who will let it gently shine into their souls. Our souls are raised higher and our spirits lifted by the shining countenance of God's face.

Thank You, Lord, for Your light which offers life.

> *Their kings will be greatly afraid, and their*
> *countenance will be troubled.*   —EZEK. 27:35

Even as the Lord lifts up His countenance upon His own, we need to allow our faces to witness to the world of His grace and glory. This often requires courage as it may mean putting aside our own troubles for the sake of others, to carrying on in hard times, and not faltering in our march toward God.

Rudyard Kipling's grand poem "If" addresses the problem of facing adversity unbowed. He advises diligence, consistency, perseverance, and basic morality. These are the things, Kipling says, that make a man.

This poet-adventurer left just one thing out of his list, the most important element of all: recognizing and accepting the Lord into our lives. No matter how much control we have over ourselves, we cannot take charge of our destiny. Only God has this ability. This is a blessing. We sometimes fail; He does not.

Bless my life, Father, that I might have an untroubled countenance reflecting Your goodness.

> *"When you fast, . . . anoint your head and wash*
> *your face, so that you do not appear to men to be*
> *fasting."*
> —MATT. 6:16–18

Religious leaders in Jesus' time made a great show of fasting, enjoying the people's admiration of their pious holiness. Jesus set things straight. Fasting is something private between an individual and God.

This wasn't the only time Jesus told His followers to keep still about their good deeds. Alms were to be given quietly, healings to be little discussed. God's reward comes to those who do His will without seeking glory.

One of the benefits of fasting is a clear mind. When the body is full, a sense of lethargy often exists. After a reasonable length fast, our minds grow alert. We see with new eyes and understand better with our hearts.

Fasting is for the purpose of coming closer to You, Lord; great are its blessings. Thank You.

He who is slow to anger is better than the mighty,
And He who rules his spirit than he who takes a
city.

—PROV. 16:32

Ruling your spirit. Keeping tabs on your temper. Slowing down your reactions so you behave responsibly instead of selfishly. These are earmarks of self-control. And they are often difficult to master for those of us who missed out on the blessing, unless we understand an important principle.

The degree of self-control you have is in direct proportion to the degree of self-acceptance you have. Put another way, if you don't value yourself, you won't tend to put any "reins" on your behavior.

In Biblical Greek, the word picture for the word *self-control* is of a horseman "pulling in the reins" on a horse. In our lives, it's a picture of our need to "pull in the reins" on a habit.

Ask yourself today, "Are there any habits or attitudes that you need to "pull in the reins" on? Like anger? Selfishness? Envy?

If we don't see our tremendous value in Christ, our self-worth won't be very high. And carrying around low self-worth is an open invitation to bad habits and a loss of control.

Thank You, Lord, that because I'm so valuable to You, I can say "no" to those things I need to.

> *Therefore, a man shall leave his father and mother and be joined to his wife.*
> —GEN. 2:25

Today's verse is used in almost all wedding ceremonies, and usually gets about as much attention as a distant relative standing in the reception line. Yet within its few words are two keys to successful relationships, especially if we've missed out on the blessing.

Did you notice the stair-step progression that must take place for a marriage to become complete? First comes leaving, then comes cleaving. We must gain independence from the past first; then, there can be a healthy interdependence.

With every couple who comes into our office for marriage counseling, we use this verse as an introductory assessment. Are they struggling with "leaving" issues (i.e., past hurts or disappointments); or from a failure to know how to cleave (from poor communication to poor conflict-resolution skills)?

Ask yourself today, "Is my marriage where it should be?" (Or, if you're single, "Are my friendships where they should be?") If not, then perhaps you need help in "leaving" some hurts from the past or in understanding the many tools that you can use to "cleave" in the present.

Lord, thank You that You can free us from the past and give us help to build a fulfilling present.

*The children of Israel could not look steadily at
the face of Moses because of the glory of his
countenance.*
                                        —2 COR. 3:7

The children of Israel could not look directly into
Moses' face when it shone because he had risen,
while communing with God, so far above them they
dared not approach. If, as Paul claimed, the ministry
of the Spirit is even more glorious, it would seem only
the consecrated will be able to endure that glory.

Christians sometimes ask for things that they could
not stand if those things came to pass. Most of us are
familiar with the stories and poems that convey what
happened when Christ answered prayers of invitation
and entered a home. Either the person who invited
Him really didn't expect Him and so wasn't prepared,
or didn't recognize Him when He came.

Our lives here are, in part, a time for us to grow so
we can one day stand before the glory of God's countenance. If suddenly thrust into His heavenly presence
without a transformation on our part, we could not
face Him. We need to be blessed with the transfiguring
power that lifts us closer to Him.

Touch my life with Your Spirit that I may be changed, Lord.

His countenance was like the sun shining in its strength.

        —REV. 1:16

Scientists continue to find out more about the glowing mass we call the sun. Its rays are being harnessed better than ever before to generate solar power and better life on earth.

Another of the hymns, written generations ago, that still appears in our hymnals is "Sun of My Soul." It expresses recognition of our dependency on God.

> *Sun of my soul, thou Saviour dear,*
> *It is not night if thou be near;*
> *Oh, may no earth-born cloud arise*
> *To hide thee from thy servant's eyes.*

There are many facets to this sparkling song. Seeing God as the sun of our souls brings thoughts of being surrounded with light; night is dispelled. The plea that no earth-born cloud may hide God from us shows the writer's discernment. Without God's light, we cannot survive.

You are the sun of my soul, Lord. Bless me with increased light.

> *"Then let our appearance be examined before you,*
> *and the appearance of the young men who eat the*
> *portion of the king's delicacies."* —DAN. 1:13

Daniel and his friends had been ordered to eat what the king was serving to the other young men he was training as his servants. Daniel pleaded his and his companions' cause with their keeper, asking that they be allowed to eat vegetables and to drink water, not wine.

Their keeper hesitated, fearing he would incur the king's wrath if these strapping young men started looking gaunt. Then Daniel asked for a ten-day trial. He and his companions wouldn't offend God by eating the king's food and were sure their faces would show continued health and strength. The Scriptures tell us what happened. They looked better and fatter at the end of the test than those who ate the king's specified diet.

What is your countenance telling others about you and God? _____

Lord, may my choices reflect You and be a witness for You.

So the woman came and told her husband, saying, "A Man of God came to me, and His countenance was like the countenance of the Angel of God, very awesome." —JUDG. 13:6

It's too bad that quite often the truly wonderful things God does are overlooked in favor of the more bizarre or spectacular such as Samson's restored strength bringing down the pillars.

Going back years before this, we find a far more gripping incident. Samson's parents had no children. Then one day, the Angel of the Lord appeared to Samson's mother and told her she would bear a son. He warned her not to drink wine or similar drinks and not to eat any unclean thing.

There is nothing to indicate Samson's mother was educated or had taken a course in recognizing holy ones. Yet she immediately ran to her husband and bore witness to the angelic ministry that had come to her. "Very awesome" was her evaluation of the visitor's countenance. It left no room for error but demanded recognition.

Our countenances should be such that others see Him in us.

May my countenance this day be filled with Your glory, God.

*And when the Philistine looked about and saw
David, he disdained him; for he was only a youth,
ruddy and good-looking.* —1 SAM. 17:42

Remember when you were young and advanced
some of your ideas to an older person? You possibly
either received interested attention, amused toler-
ance, or a you're-just-a-kid look.

Nothing destroys young people's self-confidence
more than having their dreams and ideas met with
scorn. Even well-meaning parents who love their children fall into the trap of trying to save their children
from disappointment by making them be too realistic
too soon. So what if four-year-old Jenny probably
won't become a world-famous ballerina, as she firmly
states she will? It's important for young people to have
dreams and goals.

There's nothing wrong with a response such as, "It
takes a lot of work to achieve your goal and there are
many exciting careers and choices ahead. Just stay
open and when the time's right, you'll know what God
wants in your life."

Did you have a special dream stamped out of you
years ago? The good news is: it's still not too late.
Think about it.

*Lord, bless me with the courage to believe I can still achieve many
wonderful things through Your Holy Spirit's leading.*

Abigail was a woman of good understanding and beautiful appearance.
　　　　　　　　　　　　　　—1 SAM. 25:3

The cosmetic industry would have us believe beauty comes in bottles. The billions of dollars a year in cosmetic sales show that people buy that message. From mascara to mousse, from hair brighteners to hair transplants, people focus on external appearance.

In today's verse, Abigail's beauty is linked with an equally important trait that shows an inner beauty, "good understanding." The most beautiful woman can appear ugly if she doesn't have character to match her looks. The book of Proverbs puts it this way: "As a ring of gold in a swine's snout, so is a beautiful woman who lacks discretion."

A newly mined diamond may not flash brilliantly, but its outside is deceptive. Underneath the surface is a dazzling jewel that only a gemologist or gem cutter can see. God looks at us as that gem-cutter; He can see inside our lives. If we are not consumed with adorning the outside, He will find the inner beauty reflected in "good understanding."

Father, bless me with understanding. I am beautiful through You.

There are many who say, "Who will show us any good?" Lord, lift up the light of Your countenance upon us.

—PS. 4:6

Eugene O'Neill is considered by many to be America's greatest playwright. Some of his plays reflect his sea-going days; many are sympathetic to society's outcasts. O'Neill was the first playwright to write tragedy consistently. Most of his characters searched for some meaning in their lives—love, religion, illusion.

Amidst this gloom and doom, three short sentences by O'Neill give a glimpse of deep longing: "We are broken. We live by mending. The grace of God is glue." And this from one known for his pessimism!

Ever since the fall of mankind, people have been looking to know who will show them any good. The light of God's countenance is not only good, it is the good required for us to have light, life, and joy.

Show us Your good, Lord; lift up Your countenance and light our lives.

For the Lord is righteous, He loves righteousness;
His countenance beholds the upright.

—PS. 11:7

Shortly after World War II when money became a little more plentiful in Peggy's family, her parents felt they could afford a piano. Peggy remembers going with her mother into stores that overwhelmed her.

"There sat the grand pianos, flaring and elegant, too aloof to be touched by small fingers. I tiptoed past them. Next came the new pianos, polished like mirrors. What we needed was merely a good, used piano, one in tune and in good repair.

"In the back room, dusty and crowded, we found a secondhand upright. We took it home, waxed it until it shone, and took care of it. The old upright saw us grow from childhood to adults, welcomed friends who gathered around it, and remained steady throughout all those years."

We can learn from Peggy's piano. It presented a countenance of scrollwork, not too fancy, but attractive. It sat squarely on its own feet and didn't waiver. It contained music to brighten hearts. So can we by our uprightness be His joy.

May I stand firm on my foundation, which is You, Father.

> *Why are you cast down, O my soul? And why are you disquieted within me? Hope in God; for I shall yet praise Him, the help of my countenance and my God.*
> —PS. 43:5

"Climb 'Til Your Dream Comes True" is a poem by Helen Steiner Rice. It speaks of how when we think we face insurmountable hills, things smooth out when we climb in faith. Climbing until our dreams come true incorporates believing, courage, trust in God.

What is hope other than desire plus faith? We hope for a better tomorrow so we can live victoriously in troublesome todays. Hope is beyond reason and the individual who truly loses hope, loses everything.

Hope is what helps us climb that ladder until our dreams become firm and established. It is well within reason to say that the hope that comes from having God's countenance shine on us has taken more people out of despair and defeat than any other single factor.

Is your level of hoping low just now? Hope in God and praise Him. _____

Hope is a blessing without price, Father; thank You for it.

*Blessed are the people who know the joyful
sound! They walk, O Lord, in the light of
Your countenance.*

—PS. 89:15

In our busy and noisy world, David's mention of the
joyful sound is fresh and appealing.

What is the joyful sound in your life, the blessings
you may not have seriously reflected on for a time?
The joyful sound could be laughter or a hymn, cries of
surprise and gladness, or perhaps a telephone call.
Those who have chosen Christ as their Savior know
the most joyful of sounds will be when He descends in
glory to take His own.

One of the joyful sounds with which we can bless
one another is giving testimony of what God has done
for us.

Today, look for joyful sounds. They will bless you.

*Lord, don't let me allow traffic and confusion drown out the joyful
sounds of Your creation.*

They did not gain possession of the land by their own sword, . . . but it was Your right hand . . . and the light of Your countenance, because You favored them.

—PS. 44:3

The independent, sometimes lawless, spirit that permitted early pioneers to settle the West is often remembered as the force that conquered.

This wasn't the case with the Israelites. All their swords, all their strength didn't gain possession of their land or save them from destruction. God did it because He favored them. They were the only nation that had the living Almighty God, Everlasting to Everlasting.

Today is Halloween. Children go trick-or-treating and wear fantastic costumes. Halloween is a remnant of a tradition that honored Samhain, the Celtic lord of death, and began the season of cold, darkness, and decay. The Celts believed Samhain allowed the souls of the dead to return to earth for this evening. Satanic cults even now make much of this day and rejoice in darkness. Thank God for the blessing of light and freedom from darkness our God brings!

Search out any darkness in me, O Lord, and drive it away with Your presence and light.

November

THE LORD GIVE
YOU PEACE

*Nebuchadnezzar . . . , To all peoples . . . : Peace be
multiplied to you. I thought it good to declare the
signs and wonders that the Most High God has
worked for me.*   —DAN. 4:1, 2

When Daniel interpreted Nebuchadnezzar's dream,
the king proclaimed that Daniel's God was the God of
gods, and promoted Daniel and his friends in the government. However, when Daniel's three friends refused to bow down to the golden image of the king,
Nebuchadnezzar commanded that they be cast into
the furnace.

So it was written, so it was done.

Nebuchadnezzar rubbed his eyes. How had *four*
men gotten into the furnace, and how could they all
be walking in the fire without being hurt? Why, the
fourth form was like the Son of God! In repentance and
humility, Nebuchadnezzar responded to God's protection of His servants and sent forth this blessing to all:
Peace be multiplied to you.

We need to say with Nebuchadnezzar, "I thought it
good to declare the signs and wonders that the Most
High God has worked for me." He rescues us from life's
fiery trials and keeps us unharmed in His safety.

When I walk through "firey" times, Lord, You are with me.

"And when you go into a household, greet it. If the household is worthy, let your peace come upon it."
—MATT. 10:12, 13

Jesus implied that His disciples would carry peace within themselves, a gift to be given freely to those who would accept it. For us, the crucial thought is: we as messengers of our Lord Jesus Christ must also be carriers of His peace.

In the days before telephones and telegrams and Express Mail, swift runners sped from point to point with the news. All knew they must waste no time, for what they carried was to be delivered as soon as possible.

Today, we must view ourselves as the bearers of peace in much the same way. We cannot waste time delivering our "goods" to a troubled world. Once we have peace in our hearts, we are compelled to offer it to others.

Is this a hurting time for you? A time of the loss of someone or something you hold precious? Seek your Father in prayer. He will bless you with the peace to go on and to encourage others.

_____

Father, fill me with Your peace—to overflowing.

*Then He arose and rebuked the wind, and said
to the sea, "Peace, be still!" And the wind ceased
and there was a great calm.* —MARK 4:39

The day had been long. Weary and needing rest,
Jesus got into the boat with His disciples.

Jesus fell asleep. Not so His disciples! The grandfather of all windstorms raged and beat against the
boat until it began to fill. Alarmed and frightened, the
men ran and awakened Jesus, demanding to know if
He cared that they were about to drown.

When Jesus rebuked the wind and ordered the sea
to be still and at peace, surely He also spoke to the
hearts of His disciples. He then asked where their faith
had gone and why they were so afraid. The disciples
could only shake in their sandals and wonder who this
Jesus could be that even wind and waves obeyed Him.

Those who have gone through hard times can also
run to Jesus, the source of their peace and calm during
any storm they face.

*Lord, thank You for speaking peace into my heart; for the blessing
of calm.*

"Have peace with one another."
—MARK 9:50

Joe and Glen were childhood buddies and continued to be steadfast friends. They both married and settled near one another.

One day the two men decided to go into a business partnership. Somehow, their business failed. Each blamed the other for the failure. Animosity replaced friendship.

The two men's wives were appalled. Being a little distanced from the problem, they could see blame had to be equally borne. Rather than pushing or manipulating the men, the women decided to pray.

Nothing happened for a long time. Now and then a wife would report to the other that her husband had wondered aloud how the other was getting along. The women would casually pass this on in comments like, "By the way, Marge says Glen was asking how you were, dear. He acted concerned. Billy, pass the salad to your dad, will you, please?"

Gradually the barrier began to crumble but neither man would make a move until Joe had a heart attack. Then, the first visitor was Glen, with a hearty handshake and a plea for forgiveness. Joe responded in kind.

———————

If you are harboring resentment toward anyone, ask God for the blessing of putting aside pride and restoring peace to you both.

"Guide our feet into the way of peace."
—LUKE 1:79

Near our (John's) home in Phoenix, nestled near a small mountain, is a few acres of land set aside and developed into a kind of "Jesus walk." Visitors follow a path marked with stations representing a significant time in Jesus' life, from His birth to resurrection. The tremendous benefit of walking such a path is the feeling of peace one experiences.

As we walk with Jesus, He guides us step by step into His peace. Zacharias tells us it is one of the reasons Jesus came to earth.

Ralph Waldo Emerson wrote, "What we seek we shall find; what we flee from flees from us." How true this is and how well it fits the scripture above. If we seek peace in the right place—in God—it will come. If we turn away and flee from His presence, peace will also flee from us. Seek the way of peace—now.

Guide my faltering footsteps in the way of peace, dear Lord.

*"Glory to God in the highest, and on earth peace,
good will toward men!"*
　　　　　　　　　　　　　—LUKE 2:14

The greatest historical event the world would ever know had just taken place. Jesus lay in a Bethlehem manger. An angel then appeared to shepherds announcing His birth.

Did the angels express the good will even they felt for sinful mankind at that moment, or were they referring to the birth of peace incarnate?

Some versions of the Bible record the angels' words as, "toward men of good will."

Suppose all the world was composed of people of good will. We would find life far more beautiful than we could ever imagine. God's kingdom would truly come to earth and all would be blessed. Until then, we can bring peace to our own little spot on this earth.

As I work to bring peace to others, I will be blessed with peace in my soul.

> *"But whatever house you enter, first say, 'Peace to this house.' And if a son of peace is there, your peace will rest on it; if not, it will return to you."*
> —LUKE 10:5, 6

The phrase, "a son of peace," brings many speculations. Surely a child of God should be a son of peace. Jesus doesn't say His peace cannot stay in a jangled, chaotic home, but it seems He implied peace cannot stay in an alien place.

Seasoned teachers instinctively distinguish children from happy, well-adjusted, peaceful homes and those from angry, abusive, or tension-filled families. Children from homes without peace evidence a wide range of traits that happier children only show occasionally. When children have all the problems of home to handle, and are without the skills to do so, new problems erupt at school and church. Most of the time the children don't even understand all the harm that is being done to them in homes without peace.

Perhaps you grew up in a home without peace. God can repair you. _____

Lord, may I be a child of peace.

*"Do you suppose that I came to give peace on
earth? I tell you, not at all, but rather division."*
—LUKE 12:51

It seems Jesus contradicted Himself between this
verse and those in which He promised His followers
peace through the Comforter, the Holy Spirit. On
closer examination we discover there is no disagree-
ment. The peace Jesus spoke of in John 14 as peace
the world couldn't understand has little to do with
peace on the total, sinful earth.

In subsequent verses Luke recorded that houses
would be divided with family members for and against
Him. We see this coming to pass in more modern
times. Often, individual family members hold differing
viewpoints. Unless the family comes to terms with the
differences, they will have no peace.

However, some people strive for peace at any cost.
Think of a husband or wife who worships the Lord but,
to preserve peace in the family, stays away from
church and keeps quiet about his other beliefs, even
though the need to speak causes the soul to ache. Perhaps it is to these that Jesus spoke a warning that it
wouldn't be easy to stand alone, especially in a family.
If you need strength to face this problem in your family, don't hesitate to ask God, a friend, or a counselor
for help.

_____

Bless me, God, with a strength to stand for You.

> *"What king, going to make war . . . , does not . . .*
> *consider whether he is able . . . to meet him . . . ?*
> *Or else, while the other is still a great way off,*
> *he . . . asks conditions of peace."*
> —LUKE 14:31, 32

If the hours spent bartering "conditions of peace" were directed toward solving the real ills of the world, what a different earth we would have. Instead, countries vie with one another to get what they want and to give as little as possible.

We all rejoice in the reduction of arms but this is only a step toward peace. Jesus has only one condition for His followers to obtain peace: to respond positively to His "come unto Me" call.

Once we are in His fold, we can claim the protection, peace, and joy He promised. This doesn't mean we won't experience harsh times sometimes for His name's sake. But it does mean He will walk with us. We need never be alone. This in itself brings a full measure of peace.

It's wonderful that while any peace the world makes has strings attached, the peace of God, which is beyond human understanding, is ours for the seeking.

Lord, Your precious peace is what my heart and soul need today.

The whole multitude of the disciples began to . . .
praise God . . . , saying: " 'Blessed is the King who
comes in the name of the Lord!' Peace in heaven
and glory in the highest!" —LUKE 19:37, 38

Jesus had just ridden near the descent of the Mount
of Olives. In a wave of triumph, voices took up the cry
of proclamation.

Yet in the midst of their praise lay reality. Though
they cried for peace in heaven, there has not always
been peace in heaven. We know that Lucifer rebelled
against God and took others with him. It's hard to
think of heaven as being other than a place of total
peace, but this just wasn't the case.

On the day of Jesus' entry into Jerusalem, however,
the followers of our Lord weren't thinking of Lucifer
and his band of fallen angels. Hearts swelling with excitement, caught up in the fulfillment of prophecy, they
spread their clothing on the road. How did Jesus respond? By weeping over Jerusalem, anguishing. "If
you had known . . . the things that make for your
peace!" (See Luke 19:42.)

Are we any more aware?

———————

Open my eyes, Lord, to the peace You would give me.

> *"These things I have spoken to you, that in Me you may have peace. In the world you will have tribulation; but be of good cheer, I have overcome the world."*
> —JOHN 16:33

More than seventy years ago the world went wild on this day. The "war to end all wars" was over and the boys would come home. Cymbals crashed. It was the original Armistice Day—the end of World War I.

Had not the oppressor been put down, the enemy defeated? President Wilson proclaimed November 11, "Armistice Day." Later, Congress changed it to Veterans Day, in remembrance of all U.S. veterans.

Lieutenant-Colonel John McCrae, a member of the first Canadian contingent, who died in France in January 1918, left the poem, "In Flanders Fields." (Flanders is a region of northern Belgium that saw heavy fighting.)

McCrae reminds us that those who died in the pursuit of peace throw to us the torch with failing hands. If we break faith and do not hold it high, those who lie in Flanders field shall not sleep.

We can liken this to our Christian responsibility. Even as Jesus has overcome the world, we must overcome sin and strife.

Lord, thank You for Your sacrifice that I might have peace.

"The word which God sent to the children of Israel, preaching peace through Jesus Christ—He is Lord of all—"
                             —ACTS 10:36

We've already discussed how true peace comes through our Lord and in no other way. An anonymous writer who penned these words expresses the beauty of such peace. This poem became a children's hymn.

HOW STRONG AND SWEET
MY FATHER'S CARE

How strong and sweet my Father's care,
That round about me, like the air,
Is with me always, ev'rywhere
   He cares for me.
O keep me ever in Thy love,
Dear Father, watching from above;
And let me still Thy mercy prove,
   And care for me. Amen.

Peter precedes the statement in Acts by saying that God shows no partiality. He accepts all who come to Him. The free gift of salvation is not limited to the children of Israel. It is for the world, for those who choose Him, no matter where they live. Together, we can praise the Lord of all.

We who carry Your Son's name, Lord, are blessed and can preach His peace.

> *The people of Tyre and Sidon . . . came to him*
> *[King Herod] . . . and asked for peace.*
> —ACTS 12:20

Peter was in Herod's prison. When an angel released the manacles from his hands and told him to arise, he obeyed, even though he thought it was a vision. They left the prison grounds and the angel disappeared.

By then, Peter knew he had been delivered from Herod and he went to the home of Mary, mother of John Mark, where Jesus' followers were praying. There, the servant girl Rhoda was so happy to hear his voice, she left Peter standing at the gate when she rushed in to announce his arrival. When they finally opened the door, Peter told them to keep silent and left.

Lord, many people are imprisoned by fear and need freedom as Peter did. May we know Your peace.

*To all who are in Rome, beloved of God, called to
be saints: Grace to you and peace from God our
Father and the Lord Jesus Christ.* —ROM. 1:7

In our busy world, we don't take the time for long
greetings in our letters. The apostles, however, started
each message to the saints by using a greeting similar
to this one.

It's a lesson to read just the first few lines of each
letter. They follow the same general format. First, an
identification of the writer as one who is a servant of
the Lord. Then a specific recognition of those to whom
the message was directed.

Wouldn't it be wonderful to receive a letter that began something like this:

"Terrence Radcliff, a servant of our Lord Jesus, to Mar-
ian Pearson, beloved of God. Grace to you and peace from
God our Father and the Lord Jesus Christ."

Such a blessing to read these affirmative words and
feel a true blessing given to us by both God and the
sender!

*May I be more conscious of small ways to bless others, Lord, even
in the way I greet my friends.*

Now may the God of hope fill you with all joy and peace in believing, that you may abound in hope by the power of the Holy Spirit. —ROM. 15:13

The God of hope is the God of sanity and reason. How could we go through hardships, pain, and loss without hope?

Not only that, but the hope God personifies is no mean, small wish, built on little more than a vague dream. Paul desires that those who read his letter *abound* in hope—that they be flooded with hope, from the tip of their toes to the top of their heads. Hope galvanizes people to great heroism and mighty efforts; it brings out their best.

Time after time, we read accounts of those who held on and conquered terrible difficulties. Rudyard Kipling's narrative poem "The Explorer" tells the story of one who followed what Kipling called the everlasting whisper. Hope kept the voyager going through incredible obstacles until he reached the land beyond the mountains and deserts—and found it good.

This is what hope can do for you.

God, thank You for the undying hope You have planted in my soul.

God has called us to peace.
—I COR. 7:15

Jeanne felt privileged when she received an invitation to a banquet where international peace would be discussed. As a strong Christian, she longed for world peace and viewed the banquet as an opportunity to learn how to help bring it about.

When Jeanne took her place at the long table, she picked up a small object in front of her plate. It was a stick about six inches tall and pointed at the top. Each side of the stick carried an inscription. Jeanne could only read the side that was in English. It was a wish for world peace.

The speaker said that in some countries the custom is to have peace poles. Unlike totem poles that tell a story through carved images, peace poles merely speak of peace.

God has called us to peace, to active peacemaking, to spread His peace to *our* world even when we cannot go to the *whole* world. We probably don't have peace poles sitting in our yards but maybe it wouldn't be a bad idea! We need to claim God's peace and pass it on.

I cannot give peace to others, Lord, until I receive Your blessing of peace in my own life.

> *For God is not the author of confusion but of*
> *peace, as in all the churches of the saints.*
> —1 COR. 14:33

Too many times family members, especially children, are confused by what they perceive to be mixed signals from others. The truth is obscured by what one thinks another is feeling or thinking.

To four-year-old Greg, nine months of waiting for the new playmate his mother and father promised him seemed like nine years. Finally, the day came and he had not one, but two baby sisters! Greg wasn't loved any less than before, but his home life changed drastically. As the girls grew, people exclaimed over the twins but paid little attention to their brother who also needed praise. Greg became confused.

Years later, after attending a seminar on the blessing, Greg realized he needed to deal with his feelings of insecurity. He shared his concern about having missed out on some of the family love he had needed. His mother burst into tears. She had always thought it might bother him, but hadn't known how to approach him. Talking about it brought deeper unity than the family had known for years.* If you are confused and need peace, seek your Heavenly Father.

This a world of confusion, Lord; help me to find Your peace.
*The Blessing, Chapter 10

*For He Himself is our peace, who has made both
one, and has broken down the middle wall of
separation.*
—EPH. 2:14

Yesterday we discussed how easy it is to fall victim
to confusion when we don't understand another's
words or actions. We tend to build walls between ourselves and others, shutting ourselves in and others out.
If we are to have God's peace, we must begin to tumble
down those walls.

It is impossible to keep a wall erect against even the
worst enemy if we consistently carry that person to
God in prayer. The past mistakes and offenses, which
once loomed sky high, dwindle when honest concern
on another's behalf enters in. This is why sickness and
misfortune sometimes act as a catalyst for reuniting
people.

Christ is our peace. He makes us one in spirit and
truth when we accept Him and honestly strive to follow His commandments.

Is there an existing wall in your relationship with
another that needs to be broken down by Christ, our
peace.
_____

Thank You, God, for shattering walls that divide.

And He came and preached peace to you who were afar off and to those who were near.

—EPH. 2:17

Ever since Jesus set the example by coming and preaching peace to all who would listen, His followers have endeavored to do the same. Along dusty roads, through mountains and valleys, across deserts, and in city streets, the gospel of peace is carried. Early missionaries went afoot or rode donkeys. Today's missionaries use many forms of transportation and communication to proclaim the good tidings of peace to people in foreign lands.

Others preach peace closer to home. One lady prays every time before she boards a bus that God will lead her to someone who needs a witness of His peace and love. She pauses at the front, glances over the empty seats and chooses one next to the person she feels is the person for her to approach. She doesn't push but she does share a testimony of what Jesus has done in her life. She concludes with a smile and "He loves you, too. Have a good day." Are you preaching peace every day of your life?

We can't all be like the bus lady, Lord, but bless me with the opportunity and ability to preach peace with my life.

Keep the unity of the Spirit in the bond of peace.
—EPH. 4:3

A certain white-haired lady always sat in the second row, next-to-the-center-aisle seat, for church services. Week in, week out, the dependability of her being in that spot provided stability to the congregation.

One Sunday a man came to that church for the first time. He had never met the lady. Yet as he glanced her way, something about her silver hair and her presence, made him realize she had a deep, close, genuine walk with Christ. After a long time of going to that church, he told her how he had felt the first time he saw her.

The saintly woman's eyes filled with tears. She had secretly wondered if she contributed anything to the church except in money and testimonies. Now to have this beloved friend reaffirm her worth meant a great deal. It reinforced what her family and others who knew her well had always told her.

———

God reaffirms our worth, often by using others to bless us. Can you find someone today whom you can bless in this way?

The peace of God, which surpasses all
understanding, will guard your hearts
and minds through Jesus Christ.   —PHIL. 4:7

A favorite hymn is "The Haven of Rest." In it, the author says he will sail through the stormy seas no more because he has found a haven of rest and anchored his soul in Jesus.

Few Christians escape life's storms, yet Paul said we can have God's peace. This peace will guard our hearts and minds through Jesus Christ.

It is significant to note that the promise is peace for both heart and mind. How many times do we feel our mind is at rest, only to discover we still have a troubled heart? How many times when our heart knows something is right, does our mind rise up to dispute that knowledge? Satan delights in troubling our hearts and our minds. He knows that as long as he can do this, we will never have the peace of Jesus Christ, nor the strength to move on.

It is wise to recognize that even though Satan has written the book of war, discontent, and trouble, God is the author of peace.

I know, Lord, You want to bless me; guard my heart and mind.

*Glory, honor, and peace to everyone who works
what is good, to the Jew first and also to the Greek.
For there is no partiality with God.*

—ROM. 2:10, 11

On November 22, 1963, the world was stunned by the assassination of President John F. Kennedy. Disbelief, anger and shock swept the country like a mighty tidal wave of evil.

Imagine how the disciples felt when Jesus was crucified. Surely they experienced, many times over, the shock we felt. Anyone who had ever encountered Jesus must have shared their disbelief, shock, and grief.

There is no partiality to grief. Neither, according to Paul, is there partiality with God. It has jokingly been said, "God is an Equal Opportunity God." This scripture bears it out. There is glory, honor and peace for everyone who draws near.

How comforting to know that God's love and mercy are great enough to encompass the world and enfold all who seek Him and do His will. We can be glad for God's graciousness.

Thank You, God, for Your sweeping love and goodness.

> *Therefore, having been justified by faith, we have peace with God through our Lord Jesus Christ.*
> —ROM. 5:1

A popular missionary hymn, "We've a Story to Tell to the Nations" has inspired a century of saints. It is significant that its author, Colin Sterne, could write words in 1896 that are even more relevant to the 1990s.

> *We've a story to tell to the nations,*
> *That shall turn their hearts to the right,*
> *A story of truth and mercy,*
> *A story of peace and light.*

It goes on to say we have a song, a message, and finally, a Savior to bring to the nations of the world that "all of the world's great people might come to the truth of God."

Who can sing this magnificent hymn without a lift of heart, a surge of hope, a thrill of expectancy for the day when the world will find and accept the peace of God because people have been justified through faith?

By faith we are justified, Lord; Your peace goes before us.

To be spiritually minded is life and peace.
—ROM. 8:6

How can a Christian be spiritually minded while living in an "R" rated world?

There is a story told of a small, white flower that God chose to plant in a coal mine. The flower protested, hating the idea of having to spend its life in such a dirty, black place. But God promised to make its blooms so white and pure, not even coal dust could stick to them. He also told the flower it could do far more good blooming in that dark environment than if it joined its brother and sister flowers in gardens. Content, the small, white flower thrived in the place God put her.

We have God's promise, as recorded by Paul, that when we keep our minds on the spiritual, we will have life and peace. Even as the flower rose above its sordid surroundings, so can we cling to His promises to keep us pure.

———————

Thank You, Father, for the blessing of life and peace.

> *"How beautiful are the feet of those who preach the gospel of peace, who bring glad tidings of good things!"*
> —ROM. 10:15

It is easy to picture the dusty, sandaled feet of Jesus when we read this scripture. How many weary miles did He travel in His three years of preaching the gospel of peace and of bringing glad tidings? Although He never went long distances from His home, He did crisscross the land and leave behind Him many rejoicing people.

Contemporary times bear stories of the gratefulness of those in isolated communities when a true servant of Jesus Christ comes bringing those tidings of peace through the gospel. In turn, missionaries maintain they were the ones most blessed when those with whom they labored turned from pagan gods to Jesus Christ.

All of us love to get good news. Yet there is no better news than that of Jesus' love. Are you sharing the blessing of glad tidings?

Glad tidings of good things are ours, O Lord!

The kingdom of God is not eating and drinking, but righteousness and peace and joy in the Holy Spirit.
—ROM. 14:17

Sometimes people who don't know the Lord equate Christianity with charitable organizations that feed the hungry, especially at Thanksgiving and Christmas.

In 1879, Washington Gladden wrote "O Master, Let Me Walk with Thee."

O Master, let me walk with Thee in lowly paths of service free;
Tell me Thy secret; help me bear the strain of toil, the fret of care.

Help me the slow of heart to move by some clear, winning word of love
Teach me the wayward feet to stay, and guide them in the homeward way.

Teach me Thy patience; still with Thee in closer, dearer company,
In work that keeps faith sweet and strong, in trust that triumphs over wrong.

In hope that sends a shining ray far down the future's broadening way
In peace that only Thou can'st give,
With Thee, O Master, let me live.

May I daily experience the peace only You can give, Lord.

Let the peace of God rule in your hearts, to which
also you were called in one body; and be thankful.
—COL. 3:15

Karen finished reading Colossians 3:15 and quietly laid her Bible on the table. If only the peace of God could rule in her heart! It seemed impossible. Between a full-time job, two teenagers, a husband whose business kept him away too often, and an unplanned baby, the chance for peace seemed nonexistent.

Over the next few weeks, Karen continued to think about the verse. She began to long for it to take root. Why, if God's peace did rule her, surely she could better discipline her children and control her home!

However, she knew she couldn't do it alone. That night she called her husband and asked him, for the sake of their home life, to consider changing jobs, even if it meant a cut in pay.

Next she tackled her teens. She confessed how much the chaos in their home disturbed and tired her. She enlisted their help—which they gladly gave once they realized that "invincible Mom" had her weak times, too. Eventually, Karen's husband did change jobs, and together the family grew more at peace.

God, when Your peace rules in my heart I am indeed thankful.

> *"Now when He said to them, 'I am He,' they drew back and fell to the ground."*
> —JOHN 18:6

In the Old Testament, Moses was given the all-powerful name of God when he asked, "Who shall I say sent me?" The Lord said, "Tell him [Pharaoh], 'I am' . . . sent you" (Ex. 3:13–14). The name was powerful, a "memorial to all generations" (Ex. 3:15).

Surrounded by a mob of vigilantes, Jesus quoted that same, powerful name, and His would-be captors "fell to the ground." The Greek term used to express this action was one used for wrestling matches in the Olympics. A literal translation might read that they were pinned to the ground!

Jesus body-slammed that entire, illegally-called posse with two words. Just in His voice, the hardened group of soldiers caught a glimpse of His might and power, and it pinned them face down in the dust. No one took Christ's life from Him. Only after He released them were they able to lay hands on Him.

That's the kind of power your Best Friend has. That's right. The One who loves you the most, who laid His life down for you, did it voluntarily because you are of great worth to Him. Now that's a reason for thanking God for the blessing of new life He gives us!

Lord, when I'm prone to fear, help me to realize Your power and Your love for me.

> *Now may the Lord of peace Himself give you peace*
> *always in every way. The Lord be with you all.*
> —2 THESS. 3:16

Ｗhat a beautiful blessing for a people such as we who are always in need of peace. Sometimes ministers use this as a benediction for their congregations.

In the sixties, "Peace" became the slogan among those who protested a world of war. It was overused until its real meaning was obscured. Peace is more than a byword. Peace is more than a refusal to make war. The Lord Himself holds peace in His hand.

Earlier this year we looked at blessing blockers, those things that get in the way of our receiving God's best gifts. Another blessing blocker can be ourselves. When God's peace is presented, we can be blind to its presence if bent on having our way. Seeking God and asking for specific guidance brings the kind of peace Paul describes.

Peace always, in every way, is my prayer, O Lord.

Pursue peace with all people, and holiness, without which no one will see the Lord. —HEB. 12:14

Centuries ago the founders of the United States sought "life, liberty and the pursuit of happiness" for all. More recently, some joker quipped, "We're all entitled to life, liberty and the happiness of pursuit."

Both versions imply that the pursuit of something brings rewards in itself. We've all experienced in one form or another the excitement and joy of pursuing something: good grades, a goal, our mate. The vital thing about pursuing what we want is the perseverance we learn.

When Paul speaks of pursuing peace with all men, he doesn't stop there. He goes on to add, "and holiness, without which no one will see the Lord." As we pursue holiness, we will grow in our love for God, which will increase our love for others and our ability to be at peace with them.

Father, bless me in these pursuits.

December

THE CHOICEST
BLESSINGS

> *"He also brought me up out of a horrible pit,*
> *Out of the miry clay,*
> *And set my feet upon a rock,*
> *And established my steps."*
> —PS. 40:2

I (Gary) can remember the lowest time in my life. I'd just left a job I'd spent years pouring myself into day and night. But in what seemed like an instant, I'd seen all that effort go up in smoke. Yet today, I can see that that difficult time was really the best time in my life.

All those years I worked on that job, I realized that my hopes for fulfillment were pinned to the people I worked with, the places I went, and even the things that job brought me. I thought those things would bring me what I wanted most—love, peace, and joy. But instead of the rest my soul longed for, I ended up experiencing near-daily bouts with fear, anger, and worry—the very emotions I was trying so hard to avoid! Only when I hit bottom did I realize fully that I had been looking at the "gifts" of life as the "source" of life.

People, places, and things were never meant to give us life. God alone is the Author of a fulfilling life. He fills our cups, and then, people, places, and things become the overflow. What freedom! And what security to have our feet resting securely on the Rock of Ages!

Thank You, Lord, that my security rests on the Rock, not on shifting sand.

> *"If you ask anything in My name, I will do it."*
> —JOHN 14:14

This verse has caused confusion through the ages of Christianity. Some have claimed it to ask all kinds of things, from personal riches to salvation of a loved one, or for others' success. Then, they have turned away when God did not give them what they demanded.

It is well to consider the context of this verse before taking sides concerning its message.

Jesus was speaking to a select group. He had gathered about Him those disciples who, though they did not completely comprehend Him, had left all to follow. Judas had already left the room. This was a promise Jesus gave to the little band of men who would be responsible for carrying on once He was gone.

Jesus followed up the promise. And He gave them the Holy Spirit to fill them and give them strength.

Jesus still promises to do things we ask in His name. As His disciples, we need to ask according to His will.

Father, thank You for hearing and answering my prayers.

*"The Father . . . will give you another Helper, that
He may abide with you forever—the Spirit of truth."*
—JOHN 14:16, 17

Just a little while before Jesus makes this statement, Thomas asked how they were to know where Jesus was going.

Think of the first time you remember your mother or father going away somewhere and leaving you behind when you wanted to go with them. Throughout our lives we experience the pangs of parting, sometimes temporarily, sometimes when loved ones walk around the bend in the road before us.

Jesus knew how sad and lonely His friends would be. He promised them another Helper, the Spirit of truth who would fill the God-shaped hole in their lives with comfort and the ability to go on with the work He'd entrusted to them.

He still offers this Helper, to dwell in our sad and lonely and broken hearts, to whisper, "Carry on. I am here for you."

Thank You, Lord, for the presence of Your Spirit in me.

> *"If anyone loves Me, he will keep My word; and My Father will love him, and We will come to him and make Our home with him."* —JOHN 14:23

There's a lot of excited anticipation over the arrival of a much loved guest. Everyone pitches in to spiff up the guest's room. Special meals are planned, furniture waxed and flowers arranged. The moment draws near, then, "She's here!" Warm hugs greet the loved one.

Jesus promised His disciples that if they loved Him, He and His Father would make Their home with them. Further, He broadened the promise to *anyone* who loved and kept His word.

We don't always consciously think of the heavenly guests who abide within our hearts. If we did, wouldn't we spend more time polishing and waxing and preparing the nicest accommodations we could offer?

Lord, I pray You will find pleasure in dwelling with me.

"Peace I leave with you, My peace I give to you; not as the world gives do I give to you. Let not your heart be troubled, neither let it be afraid."
—JOHN 14:27

Did you ever stop to think that a great percentage of our worst troubles stem from fear? One of God's richest blessings is peace and freedom from the crippling fear that tears us down.

Years ago a newspaper story told of a young man who saw two children dumped into a lake when their rowboat overturned. This man had a deathly fear of water. He had never learned to swim because he couldn't stand having his face underwater. Yet the sight of those children crying for help sent him plunging into the lake with a cry of his own, "God, help me, for their sake."

God heard and answered that prayer. The young man somehow got the children to safety. When reporters questioned him, he gasped, "I can't swim," and passed out. He risked his life to save the children. He had conquered fear because he stepped out in faith.

Free me from fear and a troubled heart, Father.

"In My Father's house are many mansions; if it were not so, I would have told you. I go to prepare a place for you." —JOHN 14:2

Earlier we talked about preparing our earthly homes for special visitors and how we can keep our hearts prepared for Christ's return. Now we see the other side of things. Jesus is busily making ready the places *we* will occupy. Is there just as much anticipation and joy over our coming as we experience while waiting for our loved ones? Certainly! The angels themselves rejoice and wait for the arrival of the saints.

The words *many mansions* give a feeling of spaciousness. No crowded, shabby tenements. No jammed together apartments. Instead, mansions, more beautiful than the most active imagination can picture.

Yet beyond all this is the best blessing of all: The Father and Son and Holy Spirit will be welcoming us to our new homes and we will live in Their presence forever.

This life with all its peaks and valleys is a spark in the everlasting light that is without beginning or end.

Living with You, Lord, both here and throughout eternity, is what makes everything worthwhile.

"For the Son of Man will come in the glory of His Father with His angels, and then He will reward each according to his works." —MATT. 16:27

Have you ever considered that one of the richest blessings we receive from the Lord is that of being individually rewarded for what we have done with the life He gave us?

When the time comes for all to give an accounting, each of us will stand or fall according to our works, not someone else's.

Sometimes we hear stories of how innocent bystanders get caught in a police net, are accused and convicted because of being in the wrong place at the wrong time. It isn't like that with God. He knows the truth and looks at our hearts. He sees our struggles and feels our pain. He reserves the right to set the time when His Son will return in power and glory, accompanied by angels, to gather His own.

A phrase that is familiar in modern society is, "judged on its own merit." This implies that a product is sound and reliable and able to stand by itself, rather than gaining popularity because of comparison with others. We will also be judged on our own merit and given our reward.

———

Thank You, God, for seeing and rewarding acts of love.

For the message of the cross is foolishness to those who are perishing, but to us who are being saved it is the power of God. —1 COR. 1:18

The Old Rugged Cross," written by the Reverend George Bennard, is a hymn that continues to inspire. It reminds us of how the cross symbolizes God's eternal love for humanity.

Paul tells the Corinthians that those who are perishing believe God's message is foolishness. That would be like a person standing on a sinking ship who scorns the lifeline thrown to save him. Instead of accepting the rope and being drawn to safety, he stands with crossed arms, stares at the rope and mutters, "Foolish to think such a thing can make a difference."

How different a view is given to those who trust the Lord and believe in His word. When we accept the message of the cross, the power of God enables us to conquer sin and death and every human trouble. Once we've opened ourselves to Him, it is hard to understand why others do not. We can bring blessing to their lives through the power God gives us.

Lord, help me to throw lifelines to those who are perishing.

Though I speak with the tongues of men and of angels, but have not love, I have become as sounding brass or a clanging cymbal.

—1 COR. 13:1

Paul firmly states that to be without love is to be a noisy, bothersome person.

Think of a concert you have attended where the brass section was tuning up when you arrived a little early. Did you want to clap your hands over your ears and drown out the discord? Each instrument hit different notes. Nothing blended.

Without love, we become like the noisy brass section. We create discord in relationships with other people and become difficult to be around.

Unfortunately, all their loud pushing doesn't often endear them to those they attempt to direct.

If the energy in those people could first be grounded in love, how blessed those around them would be.

Lord, help me to not be an inharmonious part of Your great orchestra, but to be filled with love.

And now abide faith.
—1 COR. 13:13

It's too bad some of the expressive biblical language isn't used more often now. Except when we sing "Abide with Me," the word *abide* is seldom heard, except in Scripture readings. Yet it is a heartwarming word, one deserving of our use.

Other words for abide are *sojourn* and *dwell*. When applied to faith, how comforting to know that it can and will sojourn and dwell with us.

When life hits hard and we reel from blows, we often feel our faith is weakened. It really isn't. A faith that has taken up long-term residence in us won't be easily evicted, even by the most adverse circumstances. Instead, it will dig in more firmly and entrench itself like a battalion preparing to do battle. One day when we've worked through the things that trouble us, that faith will rise in even stronger force.

"Footprints," is a story-poem in which God carried an individual when the way became rocky. It's a beautiful reminder that our faith does abide, if we allow it to do so.

May faith abide in me this day, Heavenly Father.

And now abide . . . hope.
—1 COR. 13:13

When God created us, He placed within us not only faith that would abide, but hope. When trouble hits, human nature strives to be in control. As long as there is any chance of handling things ourselves, we want to do just that. When true adversity comes and we are helpless to accomplish what we long to do, our inborn hope rises to the forefront. It turns back to the God who gave it, seeking relief from situations that we can no longer direct.

"All we can do is hope for the best," is a sentence used to describe the feelings of those waiting to hear from disaster areas and loved ones in danger. The more we allow hope to abide in us, the more it can swell and grow until we are filled.

Thank You for creating hope, Lord; without it, I am miserable.

> *And now abide faith, hope, love, these three; but the greatest of these is love.* —1 COR. 13:13

According to legend, Albrecht Dürer, the most famous painter and printmaker in the history of German art, did a brush drawing, titled *Praying Hands,* to honor the sacrifice and love of a friend. The story maintains that Albrecht and another painter lived together. They needed money to study and live so the friend offered to work until Albrecht could earn money with his painting. Then it would be his turn to study.

Most of us won't have the opportunity to do such a dramatic thing for another. Yet each day we have chances to show our love in a variety of ways. You can find real blessings by blessing someone near you.

Father, help me realize the greatness of Your love for me.

*"I have given you [Solomon] a wise and
understanding heart."*
                          —1 KINGS 3:12

For centuries, Aesop's fables have delighted readers.
Their pithy, allegorical humor not only offers a good
laugh, it points to special truths.

One that shows Solomon-like wisdom is of a bird
nesting in a wheat field. She advised her young to listen to what the farmer said and repeat it to her when
she returned. This was so she might know when the
family must leave to escape the reapers.

Her young grew alarmed when the farmer said he
must call the neighbors to help and then said he must
call relatives to help. The wise bird soothed their fears.
Not until the farmer told his *son* they must not wait for
neighbors or relatives, but begin the harvest themselves, did she move her family.

Wise men and women know there are things in life
that cannot be left to even the best friends. Chief
among them is developing the wisdom of and a relationship with Jesus.

*Father, bless us with wise and understanding hearts, that we may
better serve You.*

*For You have made him most blessed forever; You
have made him exceedingly glad with Your
presence.*
—PS. 21:6

David knew well how patient, kind, and merciful the
Lord was. And he spoke of the exceeding gladness he
had in dwelling in God's presence.

During our lives, the moments when we feel God's
presence most strongly are those when we are most
blessed. Some experience God with a feeling that their
hearts might burst with joy and praise. Still others experience His presence as a quiet, peaceful influence.

If you aren't satisfied that you are receiving enough
of God's presence in your life, you can:

• *Seek it* through study, worship, and prayer;

• *Prepare for it* by laying aside other things;

• *Expect it* and watch for answer of prayer;

• *Recognize it* with an openness to His plan.

*Thank You, God, for helping me to be most blessed with Your pres-
ence.*

For through Him [Jesus] we both have access by
one Spirit to the Father.   —EPH. 2:18

Before Kerry went to work for a company that manufactures parts for classified defense weapons, she underwent a series of security checks. Her first day on the job consisted mostly of extensive tours. She also received various codes and cards that would allow her access into computer systems and special storage areas.

Her brain whirled with the security checks and balances. Finally, her new supervisor told her, "Our ultimate security is that only one man, the company president, has the knowledge of the completed product. Others can see parts of the project; only he can view and control the finished plans."

This is very much what Paul wrote to the Ephesians. Paul didn't have card access to high-risk security areas. He did have—as do we—access to God, the Father, through Jesus, by the Holy Spirit. As the company president is the only access to full information concerning the company's product, Jesus is the One and Only access to our Heavenly Father. Surely this access is one of the choicest blessings God offers to His children.

———

Thank You, Lord, for making it possible for me to come to You, through Jesus.

> *Through [our Lord Jesus Christ] . . . we have access*
> *by faith into this grace in which we stand, and*
> *rejoice in hope of the glory of God.*
> —ROM. 5:2

Today, let's think about another access that is ours because of the sacrifice of Jesus. People who are issued passcards to withdraw money from cash machines have a certain faith in their card. We expect that if we insert a passcard and punch in the right numbers, cash will come out.

Without faith in a passcard, why would any person go to a cash machine? Paul says faith is necessary to receive grace, as well. Those who believe receive salvation by grace and the ability to rejoice as we hope in the glory of God.

How long has it been since you used a bank cash passcard? How long has it been since you really thought of faith as your passcard to grace? It's worth considering and reconsidering this blessing.

Increase my faith, Lord, that I may rejoice in hope.

God is my strength and power, and He makes my
way perfect. —2 SAM. 22:33

After the death of her young daughter, a mother re-lied heavily on the Scriptures to help her heal. She found that the Lord often used friends to give her strength-renewing passages.

Today's verse is one of Lee's favorite. She carries it in her heart and shared it when God took a friend's mother home.

What a blessed promise of hope! What an assurance that no matter how empty or lonely or sad we feel, it is all part of God's perfect way.

Most of the time, we do not see our way as being anywhere near perfection. The mountains and valleys are too steep and too deep for us to have a good per-spective. Remembering that God is our strength brings us peace and inspires us never to give up.

Lord, I don't always understand Your perfect plan, but I trust You for my strength.

You number my wanderings; put my tears into
Your bottle.
—PS. 56:8

If you ever wonder how precious you are to God, consider this verse. While God isn't a computer that tracks and stores everything that happens, He does keep track of our wanderings. He also puts our tears into His bottle. Does He save them as evidence of our sadness and joy?

Tears relieve the pressure that builds up in us. Tears aid in healing. At times, we wonder where they come from and how they can continue to be manufactured. Shouldn't a million tears empty us of our reserve?

Children are natural. They cry when they need to. Adults, on the other hand, are expected to control their tears. Yet doing so can stifle the freedom that comes after a good cry.

It may sound strange, but the ability to cry is a special gift from God. Remember Jesus weeping on occasion? He had no need to prove He was emotionless by refusing to show how He felt. How precious His tears must have been to His Father, the same Father who sees our struggles and has compassion upon us.

_____

Bless me, Father, with the gift of healing hurts and hearts.

"It shall come to pass that before they call, I will answer; and while they are still speaking, I will hear."

—ISA. 65:24

In the Old Testament, it is recorded that pagans went through all kinds of dancing and contortions for a sign from heaven that their petitions had been heard by their gods. Once the noise and action ceased, these believers felt the gods would shower them with the sought for blessings. If not, then the gods were angry.

Compare this bondage to images with our God. Isaiah states that before we ever call on Him, He is already answering! While we are yet speaking, God is listening. No putting us on hold while He pays attention to someone or something else. We have no need to dance and shout. He is already giving us His undivided attention, given simultaneously to all who approach Him.

To worship such a God is surely one of the greatest blessings we can ever receive. We know that when our hearts are so filled words won't come, that God's answer to our unspoken prayers is already winging toward earth.

God, You are so great. I humbly bow before You this day.

> *The word of the Lord is proven; He is a shield to all*
> *who trust in Him.* —2 SAM. 22:31

Countless followers of the Master since David's time have spoken this truth. In the first chapter of his best-selling book, *Angels: God's Secret Agents,* Billy Graham explains that he wrote the book because "God has provided Christians with both offensive and defensive weapons. We are not to be fearful . . . distressed . . . deceived . . . intimidated. Rather, we are to be on our guard, calm and alert." (Doubleday & Co., Inc. 1975)

Sounds quite similar to David's likening the Lord to a shield, doesn't it? A shield is both an offensive and defensive weapon. It not only protects the wearer but deflects harmful objects. We can feel blessed simply by cherishing the knowledge that our Lord's way is best, and when we trust in Him, we are shielded from harm and wrong.

Shield us, please, dear Father, that we may be kept safe and strong.

*The eternal God is your refuge, and underneath are
the everlasting arms.*   —DEUT. 33:27

When we were children and someone hurt our feelings or we skinned our knees, nothing comforted as
much as feeling Mom's or Dad's strong arms around
us. As we grew older, perhaps the feeling of their arms
surrounding us became more symbolic. Quick hugs or
phone calls may have replaced the encircling, but the
feeling of family still supported and encouraged us.

For many years Allstate Insurance has advertised
themselves as the "Good Hands" people. This is good
salesmanship. When we are in good hands, we feel secure and trust those hands to support and protect us
the way we expected our parents' love to sustain us.

The Bible says that God is our eternal refuge. What
a comfort! Just as our parents' strong arms often kept
us from falling, God's everlasting arms form a sturdy
net under us. Occasionally, even the best parent may
drop a child who squirms or thrashes around. God
never does. All our restlessness can never disturb
those everlasting arms that hold us.

My security is in You, Lord, and Your everlasting arms beneath me.

*You alone are the Lord; You have made heaven, . . .
earth and everything on it, the seas and all that is
in them, and you preserve them all.*
—NEH. 9:6

Years ago no housewife worth anything would go
into the winter season without her pantry and cellar
filled with preserved food. Every meat, fruit, and vegetable available found its way through the preserving
process.

While God doesn't pare vegetables, core fruit, cut
chunks of meat, or make enormous kettles of marma-
lade, He does preserve all His creation. Preserving is
the means by which perishables are kept a long time
without spoiling. Much of God's creation is perishable,
especially humankind. Unless He preserves us, we
shall perish.

Once in awhile, a seal breaks on even the most carefully handled jar, causing the contents to spoil. However, the seal God puts on our hearts can never break.

Thank You, Father, for preserving and sealing me.

God is our refuge and strength, a very present help in trouble.

—PS. 46:1

William Shakespeare wrote,

That friend who serves, and seeks for gain,
And follows but for form,
Will pack when it begins to rain,
And leave you in the storm.

Throughout our lives we may have many friends. Yet blessed is the person who finds a few true and loyal friends—the kind who, like God, are our very present help in trouble.

Often our friends fall in Shakespeare's category, while others put boots and raincoats on themselves and us so we can walk through the rain together. Trying times do prove the soundness of friendship.

Help us recognize how near You are to us each day, Oh Lord.

> *"Behold, the virgin shall be with child, and bear a*
> *Son, and they shall call His name Immanuel,"*
> *which is translated, "God with us."*
>
> —MATT. 1:23

Elizabeth Akers Allen's poem, "Rock Me to Sleep" opens with a plea for time to turn back that she might be a child again for one night. Never is this wish more real, perhaps, than on Christmas Eve.

It is easy to relate our wonder and expectancy to a night long ago in tiny Bethlehem: a baby in a manger; sleepy shepherds and singing angels; wisemen following a star of prophecy.

Immanuel. God with us. With us every waking and sleeping moment of our lives, from birth to death. Jesus, the Savior—a baby whose coming would shatter tradition and throw the religious world into upheaval. Jesus, the Savior—a friend and companion to all, regardless their station in life. Jesus, the Savior—a man whose short life counted more than all the other worthy lives ever lived and put together. Can you feel the wonder of "God with us" today?

In this season of remembrance, Lord, may I come closer to You than ever before.

*For unto us a Child is born. . . . And His name will
be called Wonderful, Counselor, Mighty God,
Everlasting Father, Prince of Peace.* —ISA. 9:6

On this day set aside to honor the birth of Christ, it is easy to wonder what happened to the peace Isaiah referred to.

Various groups, who have interpreted the Constitutional guarantee of freedom *of* religion as freedom *from* religion, actively oppose any sign of Christmas or Christianity. They're fighting a losing battle against a mighty foe: God Himself.

Throughout history there have been Christmas-Day cease fires. During the Civil War, for example, soldiers put aside arms, and joined together to sing and eat together. Starving children in war-torn countries have seen their first Christmas trees, received small gifts gleaned by homesick soldiers.

Even the sternest critic cannot deny the "something in the air" that causes people to good-naturedly wait their turn when at other times they'd be impatiently complaining. Some call it the spirit of the season. Christians call it the Prince of Peace.

Thank You, God, for the blessing of Your Son.

"There is no one like the God of Jeshurun, Who rides the heavens to help you, and in His excellency on the clouds."

—DEUT. 33:26

An old, old man sat in a rocking chair thinking of the past. A clipboard lay on his lap with a sheet of paper headed: "Those who helped me most along the way." Wavy writing betrayed the frail hand that inscribed the names of all those who had helped him through life. Heading the list was "God." Then family and friends, many long since called to their reward.

When he considered all the days of his life, he recounted times God had saved him from danger, given him strength to survive tragedy, and provided encouragement and hope to pursue his goals.

I accept and appreciate that there is no one like You, Lord.

One thing I have desired of the Lord . . . : that I
may dwell in the house of the Lord all the days of
my life, to behold the beauty of the Lord, and to
inquire in His temple.
—PS. 27:4

It seems there are two common interpretations of this verse. When Christians think of dwelling in the house of the Lord, the usual idea is of living in a heavenly house. However, David seems to have been seeking to dwell with the Lord on a daily basis—all the days of his life.

This is similar to the final verse of the Twenty-Third Psalm, "And I will dwell in the house of the Lord forever." David said many times over that the Lord was with him at all times and in all circumstances. In that sense, he was dwelling in the Lord's house.

It probably isn't as important to figure out *when* the dwelling will take place as to be sure that it *does*. Another of God's greatest blessings is the simple joy of knowing He is always near, around, above, beneath, and within us. You can claim that blessing every day of your life.

Lord, may I always make my dwelling place with You.

Weeping may endure for a night, but joy comes in the morning.
—PS. 30:5

All through the long night hours, Gregory tossed, thrashed and fought the phantoms of fear that surrounded him. *How could life have turned on him so suddenly,* he wondered.

From childhood, Gregory had found comfort in the Psalms. He slipped from the bedroom and went to his study. His mother's Bible lay open, as it always did. Gregory turned to the beginning of Psalms and began to read only those verses checked or underlined in red, a mother's loving tribute to the promises of God left for her family. He came to Psalm 30:5. "Weeping may endure for a night, but joy comes in the morning."

Gregory took a long, deep sigh and put the Bible back in its accustomed place. "If You will help me through this long night of weeping, Lord, perhaps tomorrow will be better and bring Your joy." Instead of going back to bed, the troubled man sat in a chair and watched the night shadows dissipate when touched by the early morning sun. He found the strength to go on. So can we.

_____

Thank You, God, for morning joy that will come when I endure nights of weeping.

The angel of the Lord encamps all around those
who fear Him, and delivers them. —PS. 34:7

Tommy and his sister Karen stared out the window into their wide backyard. Each night they turned away, sad, when their mother drew the drapes. After a few nights, she asked what they were looking for.

"Tents," the children chorused.

"Tents? What on earth?"

"You read to us in the Bible that angels camp all around us and take care of us if we love God," Tommy reminded her. "But we can't see the tents. Are they invisible, like the angels?"

Sometimes we're like Tommy and Karen. We know and believe that God promises He will send His angels to surround and deliver us from evil. But sometimes it would be nice to see a misty-white tent pitched beside the fence and to know that within sat an angel, on guard through the long, dark hours.

The next time you're afraid of something or some-one, picture a mighty angel standing between you and the source of your fear. Note the strength, the com-plete shield that is there to save you. Then thank God for this gift.

———————

Thank You, Father, for Your angel deliverers that are all around.

> *Behold what manner of love the Father has*
> *bestowed on us, that we should be called*
> *children of God!*
> —1 JOHN 3:1

There is created within every human being the long-ing to belong—to be loved, cherished, and accepted. When this doesn't take place in childhood, lives can be warped. Children who are taken into foster homes often find it difficult. They see themselves as second best. Adults experience this too. Sometimes second husbands or wives feel this way and wish they could have been first.

One of Christianity's great appeals to lonely people is the opportunity God offers them to belong to a fam-ily. To actually be a child of God, a beloved part of His great family is an incredible blessing. Churches that stress this aspect of God's love, and encourage their members to act toward one another as family, provide a service that can't be equaled. There is no problem that can't be overcome when we see ourselves as an integral part of the family of God. It is a humbling ex-perience to consider what manner of love our Father has for us when He invites us to be His children.

For this precious gift, Lord, I give thanks; not only in words, but by sharing this blessing with others who need it so much.

Rejoice always, pray without ceasing, in everything give thanks; for this is the will of God in Christ Jesus for you.   —1 THESS. 5:16–18

As we come to the end of another year, we need to let our hearts overflow with the remembrance of His goodness—of His blessings. An anonymous Confederate soldier left a legacy of love and hope in the words of an untitled poem. He asked for:

- strength to achieve—and received weakness, that he might learn to obey

- health to do great things—and received infirmity to do better things

- riches to be happy—and received poverty to be wise

- power to gain praise—and received weakness to feel the need of God

- all things to enjoy life—and received life to enjoy all things.

The soldier concludes that he got nothing he asked for but everything he'd hoped for. Despite himself, his unspoken prayers were answered, and among all men he was most richly blessed.

The choicest gift of our Lord and our God is our living hope of the resurrection by the One who keeps us until that day.

May I finish this year strengthened by Your power, God, and enter a new year blessed with Your abundant mercy and salvation.

About the Authors

Gary Smalley, president of Today's Family, is a doctoral candidate in marriage and family counseling and has a master's degree from Bethel Seminary in St. Paul, Minnesota. His previous best-selling books include *If Only He Knew, For Better or for Best, Joy That Lasts, The Key to Your Child's Heart.* He and his wife, Norma, are the parents of three children, Kari, Greg, and Michael.

John Trent, vice president of Today's Family, has a Ph.D. in marriage and family counseling and holds a master's degree from Dallas Theological Seminary. He wrote with Gary the best-selling books, *The Blessing, The Gift of Honor, The Language of Love, Love Is a Decision,* and *The Two Sides of Love.* He lives in Phoenix, Arizona, with his wife, Cynthia, and daughters, Kari Lorraine and Laura Catherine.